ALBERT EDWARD SPRING

NO ORDINARY MAN

By
Phil Spring
With comments by Dan Spring

MAPLE
PUBLISHERS

Albert Edward Spring: No Ordinary Man

Author: Phil Spring

Copyright © 2024 Phil Spring

The right of Phil Spring to be identified as author of this work has been asserted by the author in accordance with section 77 and 78 of the Copyright, Designs and Patents Act 1988.

First Published in 2024

ISBN 978-1-83538-167-0 (Paperback)
      978-1-83538-168-7 (Hardback)
      978-1-83538-169-4 (E-Book)

Book Layout by:
    White Magic Studios
    www.whitemagicstudios.co.uk

Published by:
    Maple Publishers
    Fairbourne Drive, Atterbury,
    Milton Keynes,
    MK10 9RG, UK
    www.maplepublishers.com

A CIP catalogue record for this title is available from the British Library.

All rights reserved. No part of this book may be reproduced or translated in any form or by any means, electronic or mechanical, including photocopying, recording or by any information storage and retrieval system without written permission from the author.

This book is a memoir. It reflects the author's recollections of experiences over time. Some names and characteristics have been changed, some events have been compressed, and some dialogues have been recreated, and the Publisher hereby disclaims any responsibility for them.

CONTENTS

FOREWORD 5

HIS EARLY DAYS 7

PRE WAR LIFE 10

THE WAR YEARS 14

THE 11TH (SCOTTISH) COMMANDO ON THE ISLE OF ARRAN 18

THE JOURNEY TO WAR 25

AND SO IN TO ACTION 30

NORTH AFRICA WITH THE LRDG & THE SAS 36

JOINING THE 10TH BATTALION THE PARACHUTE REGIMENT 52

ITALY HERE WE COME 62

THEIR SOMERBY HOME 69

OPERATION MARKET GARDEN 76

AIRCRAFT CHALK MARK 697 78

BEHIND ENEMY LINES 86

THE HAZENHOF 90

THE REMARKABLE BRAVERY OF THE AMERICAN AIRCREW 93

DOING RECONNAISSANCE 98

JOHANNES VAN ZANTEN & HIS BOYS 100

THE ESCAPE 107

RETURNING TO SOMERBY 111

WHAT NEXT FOR ALBERT 114

THE END OF THE WAR & DEMOB TIME 126

AFTER THE WAR 127

POACHER TURNED GAMEKEEPER	129
LOSING OUR MUM	136
RETURNING TO ARNHEM	139
MEETING ED FULMER & FURTHER VISITS	147
THE REMAINING YEARS	170
LOSING ALBERT	172
THE FUNERAL	175
THE AFTERMATH	178
PERSONAL REFLECTIONS	179
ALBERT'S QUALITIES	183
OUR FAMILY	185
ALBERT'S FRIENDS & COMRADES	192
OUR FRIENDS	200
ALBERT GETS A MENTION	204
ACKNOWLEDGEMENTS & BIG THANK YOUS	213
INTERESTING MEMOIRS	217

FOREWORD

My objective has always been to record the story of the life of Albert Edward Spring, my father, particularly relating to capturing his exploits as a soldier during World War II where he served as one of the original Commandos and then as a Paratrooper.

The context being that Albert was really a country boy who lived all of his life in the little village of Winwick in what was Huntingdonshire now Cambridgeshire.

We live in different times now, with different expectations, however, this is a story of a simple life shaped through extreme adversity based on good old fashioned principles.

There is a saying that everybody appears to be ordinary until you get to know their story. Hopefully, this book is a great example of just that.

There are so many other fine people intertwined in to Albert's life. Hopefully, I have done them justice. Perhaps you will understand why many of them have, like Albert, become my super heroes.

It is not intended to be a book of military accuracy. Indeed, I am sure it is not. However, it is my interpretation and understanding of conversations, readings and observations. Therefore, I apologise to those who want to be picky about times, dates and happenings.

My greatest wish is that you enjoy reading this account and you realise why I have given it the title Albert Edward Spring No Ordinary Man.

This book is dedicated to the most important people in my life: My Granny Farrer, Edward Spring, the Granddad I never knew and haven't even got a photo of, Granny & Grampy Taylor and my mum, Olive Spring, and Emma and James, my two wonderful children, Dez, Emma's partner and Olivia, James' wife, who mean so much to me along with my super grandchildren namely Martha, Ruby, Logan, Ethan, Juliette and Sienna, all of whom I love and admire so much.

And last but not least my father Albert Edward Spring without whom this book would not be possible.

I sincerely hope my children and grandchildren continue the legacy of Albert's story and the strong bond with the families of those people involved with what happened in Holland in September 1944, when my surviving brother Dan and I are not able, because it is so important to remember and cherish the gift that the likes of Albert and all those remarkable people gave us.

And finally, a little bit about me, I was born in Winwick in 1949, the youngest of the four Spring boys born. The ways of the countryside were never really for me so I joined the beloved Mitchell Construction Kinnear Group in Peterborough in 1967 and have been in property and construction business ever since. Ironically, like Albert, turning from Poacher to Gamekeeper protecting Clients from the vagaries of the construction industry.

This book came about because I was the one who arranged and took my dad back to Arnhem in 1991 and it changed my life. It has taken a long time to put all the stories on to paper. Hence I hope you enjoy the story of Albert and his family.

Phil Spring

HIS EARLY DAYS

Albert was born on 6th May 1916 to Edward and Edith May Spring and lived his early years up at Winwick Hill Cottages in the village of Winwick Huntingdonshire, near the border with Northamptonshire. It was a very small rural village of seventy to eighty inhabitants, with a pub and a shop both of which closed many years ago. To get your bearings the nearest towns are Huntingdon to the south, Oundle to the north, Kimbolton to the west and Sawtry to the east.

Albert was the youngest of three children. His siblings were Grace and John.

On 10th July 1917 tragedy struck when their father Edward Spring was killed whilst blowing up a bridge to the south of Ypres Belgium as a fore runner of the Battle of the Somme. He is buried in Spoilbank Cemetery there in the Belgium countryside which I have visited twice, once with my brother Dan and our eldest brother Peter and his daughter Melody have also visited.

My Granny Farrer has always been a super hero of mine because there she was widowed with three children aged 5 and under.

There was no state social benefits as we know it these days. If I remember correctly, Granny received her husband's war pension up to the end of World War I in 1918 or shortly afterwards, in the sum of twenty five shillings and five pence to sustain herself and the children.

After that she was on her own to fend for her family alone. What an awesome thought. We know her family, friends and neighbours certainly rallied around her and the children.

Ironically, this tragedy shaped Albert's life at a very early stage. It is said that at the age of seven he was the breadwinner, by catching rabbits with his snares and ferret and killing a pheasant with his catapult. Repeat all at the age of seven.

It must have been really tough but that is how life was in those days.

Albert attended the village school in Winwick which meant a walk of just over a mile each way in all sorts of weather.

He was a reluctant pupil who needed literally the crack of a horse whip from the farmer at the bottom of Winwick Hill to help him on his way.

Edward Spring, Albert's dad

Thanks to the excellent research by my good friend Steven Headley thus;

Albert's father Edward Spring was, unfortunately, killed in the First World War when Albert was just a baby although Edward did see his son as he managed a short term of leave before he died.

Edward and Edith were married in the Parish Church Winwick on the 19th March 1916 by the Vicar George Green. They had two days together, then Edward left for the front.

3476 Private E Spring joined the Northants 4th Battalion on 23rd November 1914, on completion of his basic training he was issued a new service number 31358 and transferred to the Northants 8th Battalion A Company and, eventually, moved to the front in France.

On 10th July 1917, he was posted missing presumed Killed in Action after being detailed to assist in the demolition of a bridge in Belgium. Edith was notified on the 3rd November 1917 of Edwards death, she may have previously been notified he was Missing in Action (MIA), the delay in notification was probably due to the time it took to confirm he had been Killed in Action (KIA).

Edith was awarded a Widows Pension of 25 shillings and 5 pence a week, this included an allowance for the children on the

3rd June 1918. Once Edwards military affairs and administration was completed, Edith received the balance of Edwards pay being £4 and 14 shillings.

A request to clarify the parentage of Albert's sister Grace as it was noted she was born on 16 December 1912 was initiated on 14th January 1918. This was followed by a request to clarify if Grace had been maintained by Edward. She was, as testified by the Vicar: "Grace was born to Mrs Spring when she was 16 and in service in Peterborough. Grace lived with her Granny till her mother (Edith) married Edward, she then became a member of his household. Edward was a soldier when he married and left 2 days after the wedding".

On the 2nd July 1918 Edward's Commanding Officer was requested to dispatch Edward's personal effects to his widow. A further request to send Edward's medals to Edith was sent on 11th December 1919. On 31st March 1958 Edith duly received the medals Edward had been awarded comprising of The British War Medal and The Victory Medal. Presumably, Edith would have received a Death Plaque inscribed with Edward's details

Edward is buried in Spoilbank Cemetery, Vaarstraat 1918, 8902 Leper, Belgium. Grave number ref Q33

Dan Spring's Response to the above

"Granny had several Missing In Action letters, and one informing her of his death. I know because she had my birth certificate and when I got around to getting married she was looking for it and found these letters, started to read them and threw one of them into the fire in tears, which I think I have one of at home."

PRE WAR LIFE

Albert showed no inclination for or love of academia and would have left school at the earliest opportunity to work on the land and take on general labouring jobs.

He married Edith Olive Taylor from the nearby village of Clopton on 15th April 1939.

They lived with Granny Farrer at Vine Cottage in the centre of the village. I say Granny Farrer (nee Spring) because she had remarried to Ernest Farrer, as needs must.

Ironically, we always knew our Granny as Granny Farrer and it never even occurred to us why. It didn't even matter as she was the most kind and gentle person that put foot on this Earth.

Her home at Vine Cottage was an old cottage that only had a cold water supply to the kitchen, no electricity supply and no inside toilet. The loo was located in a shed at the top of the garden where a torch and newspaper squares were the order of the day, with the contents being taken away every Thursday evening.

Vine Cottage was just across from the village school, which in turn was across the road from the village church. Immediately adjacent to the church is the village green next to the main B660 road. This is where we held the annual village garden fete and was our football pitch where jumpers were the goal posts. In the summer, it served as our cricket pitch. There is a tragic story of how one of the village lads was indeed killed by a cricket ball there many years previously.

There was a close link between Granny Farrer and our sporting activities on the green. We were the luckiest sport boys in the world because at half time we all ran over to raid her pantry for the most wonderful treats of homemade cakes, buns and perhaps a crumble or an apple pie, washed down with a bottle of pop with the flip top Corona bottles or more likely good old fashioned "corporation pop".

That is not a treat even enjoyed by the modern prima-donna footballers!

It didn't matter who's side you were on, as Granny treated everybody the same. She was the most kind and generous person in the world to us, who gave so much expecting nothing in return.

There was no mention of money or charging, it was all free. Granny was the greatest cook ever, using her cast iron hearth in the living room consisting of a central coal fire which provided hot water to the left and the oven to the right. The oven wall adjacent to the fire was cracked hence it was a pure art form as to how Granny achieved such wonderful baking and cooking.

Uncle Vic, her son by Ernest Farrer, lived there with his mum and he liked to go out for a few pints, particularly on a Saturday evening. Hence, one of us Spring boys would keep Granny company by staying over with her.

I can remember sitting in front of the fire, with that lovely warm glow from an open fire, either chatting away or just watching the world go by.

The fire's light was aided and abetted by the paraffin lamp in the middle of the large dining room table. Talk about serenity! This was total bliss, supported by gentle conversation with a loving granny who did not expect much from a world that had treated her so badly.

Her second husband Ernest Farrer had died in the 1950s as a result of poor health caused by his war wounds from his service in World War I.

Coming back to that kitchen table, Granny looked after one of Albert's working terriers by the name of Bill. He was one of the very best working terriers when he went to ground in search of badgers and foxes. He was number one, as tough as nails and not frightened of any person or creature.

Bill was also very mischievous and led Granny a merry dance. Two examples come to mind;

The first one being him patiently sitting with his paw up waiting for that darn mouse to appear from that little hole in the skirting. He never failed.

The second one being rather more hilarious, certainly from Bill's mischievous view point. Albert kept his pigs up in the orchard where they loved to rootle with their snouts for the walnuts from the huge walnut tree that dominated this large orchard.

Bill was always looking for the chance of the orchard gate being left open so he could get amongst them and wind up the pigs so they would chase him down the garden path. It was his dream come true!

On this particular day, such an opportunity arose and as quick as a flash, Bill took it and chased after the pigs and the sow, in particular.

The sow, in maternal protective mode of her piglets, gave chase after naughty Bill. Off he shot through the orchard gate with the sow in hot pursuit, down the garden path and in through the back door leading in to the scullery and then the kitchen / living room. It was pure mayhem all of Bill's making. That mayhem resulted in the kitchen table being tipped over.

Bill was not for giving up as he continued the chase back out of the house via the back scullery door and back towards the orchard.

That was Bill to a tee. What a character, so much so Albert in his later years wrote a book called Characters and Bill has a chapter dedicated all to himself.

Talking of the toiletry arrangements at Vine Cottage. When we stayed over on Saturday night, the bed was huge and sloped into the middle so it could be difficult to climb out. When a call of nature came it was an uphill climb to get out of bed and use the "guzunder" (the chamber pot being so named because it goes under the bed!). I suspect there are not many of those in use in the modern day home!

THE WAR YEARS

It is important to remember at the outbreak of World War II Albert was a 23 year old married man with one child, Peter, who was born on 16th November 1939. Hence he was a reluctant volunteer. Nonetheless the time came for Albert to be conscripted in February 1940.

Albert was ideal soldier material because he was tall at over six feet and very fit because he was used to manual work, biked everywhere and was a regular attendee at the boxing club in Kettering which was a good 20 mile bike ride each way at least twice per week.

His early experiences as a boy came in very handy because of his poaching exploits in the rural countryside around Winwick and the surrounding fields where he became very familiar with shot guns.

So you can imagine Albert's response when after joining the Lincolnshire Regiment, he found they did their Parade ground drills using broomsticks because there was a shortage of rifles. He was not impressed but he stuck with it.

As it happened, the Seaforth Highlanders had taken an awful beating on the beaches of Dunkirk. As a result when they regrouped they were looking for volunteers to replenish the ranks of this famous proud old Scottish Regiment.

They put up notices seeking volunteers to join them at the traditional base at Fort George just north of Inverness. Remember, that is an awful long way from home for a country boy from the little village of Winwick Huntingdonshire.

Volunteer he did, and moved to Scotland, whilst his family stayed at home with a degree of intrepidation. The loss of life at the likes of Dunkirk brought a chill to everybody's mind especially our mum Olive.

Albert may have been a country boy but he was a proud Englishman who would fight to maintain our freedom from an evil foe.

I can recall him telling me that it simply had to be done to protect our freedom and the further away from home the better.

He also told the story of when he decided to volunteer for the 11th (Scottish) Commando and came the time to leave the Seaforth Highlanders, he and others were told by the Commanding Officer, in no uncertain terms, that they had served in the best army in the world; not the British or the German army but the Scottish army. The Scots, if nothing else, were and still are very proud of their fighting tradition.

Albert, being a true Englishman, said that serving in the Scottish army brought other interesting challenges because of the rivalry between the Scots and the English.

Friday or Saturday evening could be interesting when the Scottish lads went in to town for a few drinks. There was no doubt a Scottish soldier full of alcohol was much more hostile, particularly towards their auld enemies from south of the border!

It is important to remember, that at this time, the total focus was on fighting. They trained to fight and kill twenty four hours per day. Our mum said when her husband came home all he wanted to do was fight, even if it was only the Americans based at the local airfields at Molesworth, Polebrook and Alconbury!

As Albert said "a drunken Scotsman, who you considered to be your dear friend when sober would not hesitate to run a bayonet through you upon his return from the local hostelries."

Consequently, the English did not leave the camp. They were too busy planning for their own preservation when the Scots came back from the pub.

The English lads would, subsequently, ambush their colleagues and tie them up for their nights slumber in the very same tents which were those circular ones, housing anything up to twenty two men, where everyone slept with their feet towards the centre pole.

In the morning, after a good night's sleep and with the effects of the previous evenings endeavours worn off, they then were released and everything returned to normal between the fellow soldiers

He gave his all to the Seaforth Highlanders, however, there was to be a twist of fate.

Winston Churchill wanted to form a small group of specialist fighting forces who operated totally differently to the traditional army. Churchill got his idea from when he was captured by the Boer Kommandos in the Boer War in the late 1800s.

He had never forgotten how impressed he was with them. They were not great in number but they operated in a different way. They didn't march or parade like the traditional forces. They did not wear traditional uniforms and could kill their foe in total silence without the aid of a gun. They were into guerrilla warfare, working behind enemy lines in the most audacious of manners and locations. The whole objective was to surprise, disrupt and totally unnerve the enemy.

These were the newly formed British Commandos and they were recruiting from scratch.

Once again, the posters were out looking for volunteers for these elite forces. The requirement was for volunteers for the newly formed 11th (Scottish) Commando.

Albert, with his best mate from Stamford, volunteered, as they yearned to see some action. As he said "all I wanted to do was fight the Germans because that was how this bloody war was going to be settled in the end, out there on the battlefield."

Just in case you do not know, a Commando consists of a force of 500 men; no more no less. These 500 men are split into 10 Troops of 50 men.

So how do those in charge select the 500 soldiers? According to Albert, in this case it was simple; they marched the 700 volunteers 101 miles. They chose the first 500 to complete the arduous march.

Albert and his mate had a plan. They didn't want to be amongst the first to get there because they would expect great things from them. Hence the plan was to finish in the middle of the chosen 500 which they duly did.

As a result Albert was successful in being selected to be one of the chosen few for this very proud new special elite force.

THE 11ᵀᴴ (SCOTTISH) COMMANDO ON THE ISLE OF ARRAN

The 11th (Scottish) Commando moved to the Isle of Arran, off the west coast of Scotland, to commence their training.

There were a number of other Commando units based there so as you can imagine the competition was fierce with each one trying to outdo the others.

By their very name they were always going to be unique. No ordinary name for this Commando. They were never going to be 11 Commando, no, they were Scottish and very proud of the fact. Their Commanding Officer was Lieutenant Colonel Pedder who was a true Scot from Highland Light Infantry Regiment.

They did not wear traditional berets; they wore, with particular pride, their very own Tam o' Shanter with the distinctive black hackle. No green berets for these boys. Hence the reason why my brother Dan and I never quite understand the fuss made about the Green beret in the modern day Commandos.

I understand after the war ended all further Commandos came from the Royal Marine Commandos who made the green beret their trade mark.

These lads undertook some of the most intense training ever back in 1940, endured horrendous losses on their first raid and fought in the extreme conditions in North Africa and the Middle East but, they never wore the green berets, it was always the Tam o' Shanter for them! That is the first of many unique features that set them apart.

Commandos are not like other soldiers because, for a starter, they were not provided with billets, they had to find their own accommodation in the local community. This formed a very special bond between the local communities and the soldiers.

The 11th were based in the south east of this beautiful island around Brodick and Lamlash.

I was fortunate enough to visit Arran a few years ago. It is a beautiful little island where the indigenous people are very proud of their island and its military past as a breeding ground for some of the finest Second World War soldiers this nation has seen.

For those of you who study the history of the War may recall that it endured one of the worst air crashes as part of the military supply lines of United States aircraft for the war effort.

The routine was for the brave American air crews to fly many aircraft over to Scotland in effectively air convoys, where it was relatively peaceful and quiet. When they had gathered up sufficient air crew together they would put them on a flight back to the United States to repeat the supply chain process.

Unfortunately, one such return flight aircraft hit the high ground, possibly Goat Fell, on the island and all the very brave personnel perished. A very sad and sombre day.

Goat Fell was very familiar to Albert, along with his comrades, as his early morning routine started with a run from his digs in Lamlash up to the top of Goat Fell at 874 metres / 2,876 feet above sea level, and back down and then out along the 100 yard long timber pier in Lamlash, dive into the sea, and swim back ashore where an Officer, also presumably a gentleman, instructed them to go and get their breakfast. What a start to your days' work!

If you go to Lamlash now there is no pier. However I know there was one because of my per chance meeting with Spud and Jessie Taylor, who lived in Lamlash all their lives.

After telling them the story of my dad's pre breakfast routine they duly produced a photo of the huge timber pier which also served as the mooring point for the three ships that took the soldiers to the theatre of war in January 1941. More of that later.

Jessie had been a teenager in Lamlash in 1940 up to the time of the Commandos' departure in late 1941. She worked in the local chemists shop and lived for the regular dances each weekend.

She recalled talking to some of the men way back then about seeing them kissing and cuddling as part of their training.

Some kissing and cuddling! They were actually learning how to kill a man in an instant without a sound, using the famous standard issue Fairburn Sykes dagger!

Jessie knew it as the Commando kiss and cuddle. I wonder what the unwitting enemy called it. Perhaps they never got the chance to tell!

Spud and Jessie were very kind, generous and caring people who thought the world of their military visitors during those fleeting months in the early forties.

So much so they continued to support the reunions of their beloved 11th (Scottish) Commando on the island and the larger Commando family on the main land.

Absolutely wonderful people, and indeed Jessie would ring me occasionally. Sadly she died in March / April 2022, I do miss those calls. What a wonderful lady who really understood how special these men were.

I suspect Jessie was a microcosm of the overall love, support, care and pride shown to these privileged men.

Their training was intense with yomps around the island (allegedly about 26 miles) in full kit two or three times a week regardless of wind, rain or shine or a mixture of the whole lot.

Yomping, as I understand it, is a mixture of running and marching nonstop.

The stories of the training are legendary. A typical one being when a unit of fifty Commandos were observed out on a yomp in a howling gale in full kit and as they approached the pier they marched to the end of it and jumped in the sea and swam ashore as if part of a normal days work.

These men achieved remarkable levels of fitness and endurance. No wonder Albert was considered to be the fittest person in the county of Huntingdonshire back then!

Although he, like his contemporaries, did not speak much about those days, there were a couple of funny anecdotes. The first one was when he and one or two others found themselves in a bit of bother because they wolf whistled at this beautiful lady who turned out to be the Commanding Officer's wife!

Another such occasion was as part of their marine / water skills training they rowed from Arran, for a mock landing on the mainland one Saturday evening, only to be fired at by the local Home Guard who had not been advised of such activities on this particular evening!

Albert said you have never seen them turn that boat around and get the hell out of there so quickly.

Their training was for real as they used live ammunition so there was no margin for error.

There was also frustration in him because, as mentioned earlier, all he wanted to do was fight and defeat the enemy as far away as possible. The many months of training got to Albert because what had this got to do with winning the bloody war!

How do I know this? It is simple, my great Aunty Wynn Plaister, who lived in Totnes Devon told me of the letters he wrote to her in this vain. Albert wanted to be killing and defeating the enemy and it was as simple as that.

Aunt Wynn told me of a surprise visit from her favourite nephew during those days when he had been escorting a soldier prisoner to or from the likes of South Wales when Albert took a detour to sunny

Devon. She was absolutely delighted. God rest her soul as she is long gone but she was so proud of her nephew, this very fine fighting soldier.

Albert was always a man of stature, he was the big quiet strong man who at face value took on the challenge of war and all that it brought, good and bad, with a sense of purpose.

Whilst he was never Officer material because a boy, who left the so called state secondary school system at an early age, was never going to make the grade.

He gained the respect of his fellow men in the non-commissioned ranks and, most importantly, he could be totally relied on by the upper echelons.

For a soldier of his character and ability promotion was inevitable. How do you think he achieved his first step on the ladder to Corporal whilst training as a Commando on Arran?

Could it be he did something rather remarkable, maybe a feat of strength or endurance or indeed bravery and certainly independence and reliability?

No. It all came about because of what Albert saw as a routine Saturday when he had been asked to be involved with some of the Officers who wanted a day's grouse shooting as a respite from the arduous training.

Albert, with his extensive poaching experience and ways of the wild was the ideal man. He could catch anything almost anywhere. It was a true natural gift given and honed from those tough times up Winwick Hill from a very early age.

Hence, on this particular occasion the Officers enjoyed their days shooting and, on their way back, Albert was asked to put up some rabbits as they wanted to do some rough shooting.

Albert duly put up six running rabbits, which the Officers missed, each and every one! Albert was not impressed, clearly all that weapons training these elite soldiers had undertaken had not paid dividends on this particular day.

Therefore, Albert, totally unarmed except for his stick, killed six rabbits and presented them to the Officers as an example of how it should be done!

As was the way of the army, the next morning a notice was found pinned to the cook house door announcing Albert's promotion to Corporal. We do have a photo showing him with his hard won stripes somewhere.

That was Albert to a tee. He was fiercely independent with a mind of his own. He didn't say much because his deeds did the talking for him. Perhaps the words 'strong willed' sums him up best.

He did go on to make the rank of Sergeant with the 11th, which he took with him to the 10th Battalion The Parachute Regiment when they were formed in Kabrit Egypt. Clearly, a totally reliable performer who delivered under pressure. What an accolade for a country boy of little education.

Albert had only spoken briefly about his time as a Commando either in training or the theatre of war in the Middle East and North Africa. Hence, when he passed away in 2002, he had said enough to stir the curiosity in my mind.

There it was, gnawing away at me, so after a bit of research I dropped a note to the Combined Operations website pointing out that we knew he had been in the 11th (Scottish) Commando, trained on Arran, had been on the Litani River raid in June 1941, had worked with the likes of Paddy Mayne, David Stirling (of SAS fame), Richard Pedder and Geoffrey Keyes as well as the Layforce. Also he had served with the likes of the Long Range Desert Group and possibly the SAS.

Despite knowing these headline points, we had never seen his name in writing confirming the fact. My ambition had always been to simply open a book and see my dad's name and or his picture there.

I asked for confirmation of this simple fact and at the same time, pointing out he did not talk about it other than to mention a few funny tales about the likes of Paddy Mayne.

The response I received was very straight forward. It confirmed Albert had indeed been a member of the famous 11th (Scottish) Commando and done all the things I had mentioned and went on to say that he must have been good because the 11th did not suffer fools gladly. They added he had walked amongst giants.

Can you imagine how proud I felt. I swear the hairs stood vertical on the back of my neck along with a very proud warm glow all over.

I was absolutely chuffed.

The note went on to say, "your father did not need to talk about it because he had actually been and done it with the very best and he had walked amongst giants."

What my Dad? That simple country boy!

It was one of the proudest moments of my life.

Despite the frustrations of several months of extensive training on the Isle of Arran January 1941 arrived and the training was over and it was time to go and fight.

It is important to remember that a number of the recruits had lost their lives training there. That was how tough it was.

THE JOURNEY TO WAR

Hence, in late January 1941 the three Glen boats, HMS Glengyle, Glenearn and Glenroy, left Arran carrying members of the elite 11th (Scottish) Commando and other Commando units, who were equally as good.

The Commandos would be long associated with these boats.

It was a very sad day for the people of this very proud island. As I mentioned earlier Jessie was a teenager and she said how she and many others cried because they had lost so many revered members of their wider family, who had given them so much enjoyment, excitement and above all else, hope.

These highly trained Commandos were ready for action and it was time to go and do the real business as the Glen boats slipped from their moorings on the pier at Lamlash.

This was always going to be a long hazardous journey to their final destination of Cyprus via Egypt because this was at the height of a World War and the Mediterranean was the epicentre of much tough fighting and manoeuvres involving the mightiest military hardware and forces both sides could muster.

Therefore, it wasn't a simple question of down to Gibraltar turn left and sail and dock at Cyprus. Not quite like a modern day cruise holiday leaving from Southampton and calling at all points south with the day trips ashore.

For a start, from the northwest coast of Scotland down to beyond the south west tip of England and indeed Wales was quite a trek in the winter of 1941.

The details of the journey are sketchy but they were going the very long way round via the southern Cape of South Africa then only to make their way back across the Indian Ocean then up to the southern end of the Suez Canal and beyond.

I do not know too much about the journey, although it took upwards of eight weeks but what Albert did tell me was they kept themselves fit by exercising and practising their shooting skills.

There they were the shining example of Churchill's elite forces, which were going to spearhead the downfall of Hitler and Nazism!

But he said, mockingly, nothing was further from the truth as they approached their turning point of the Cape a lot of them were violently sea sick and frankly were in a total state of distress and disarray.

Nonetheless, they smartened themselves up and put their best foot forward upon disembarking in Cape Town, for a short stop over, where they marched in formation to show off these super troops. I don't know whether this was on Churchill's instructions, given his experiences with the Boer Kommandos in that country some 50 years earlier.

These lads would have looked very impressive because they had three things going for them; one; they were handsome, two; they were fit, and three; by God, they could fight!

In later life, a trip of some seven miles or so could be a challenge, but here was this Winwick boy marching through Cape Town, South Africa, thousands of miles from the centre of his universe.

After their break to enable the replenishing of the ships and allow the men to regain their land legs, the rest of the voyage is even more sketchy but they eventually made it to their base in Cyprus with their Glen boats via Egypt.

It is important to put the whole concept of Commando forces in context with the regular British army.

The Commandos were the brain child of Churchill and the regular army did not like them because they did not behave in the conventional military manner. They were, to the established command and discipline structure, seen as unruly renegades who operated in unconventional ways.

I know it was a TV drama but just look at the recent "SAS Rogue Heroes" series of programmes and it was plain as the nose on your face these new boys on the block did not fit in with conventional military ways of doing things.

Perhaps that is why people like Paddy Mayne and David Stirling were considered to be two of the wild children of the warring world and were not to be aided, supported or tolerated under any circumstances!

It is important to remember the regular army were running the war, plain and simple. They would do everything within their power to stop or hinder these renegades.

That is the back drop to their involvement in the war effort. I never discussed it with my dad but he told us all "that the country's greatest asset was its fighting men and as such they should not be wasted needlessly and must be used effectively and with care."

I know from his reaction to the losses on the likes of the Litani River raid and later at Arnhem, he thought too many good men were lost needlessly. Perhaps this was a throwback to World War I where his father had lost his life with hundreds of thousands, indeed millions like him. What a waste.

Other than the attraction of a shilling a week danger money perhaps that is what was behind his move to the Parachute Regiment in 1943.

Those of you who knew Albert will understand what I mean. The one thing he could not tolerate was being "buggered" about, forgive the phrase but it was what he detested all his life. If he were still here now I suspect the bureaucracy would drive him crazy. To Albert a spade was not a shovel or any other digging implement, it was still a spade.

I know it saddened him when he lost so many of his comrades on the Litani River, in Palestine, Italy and North Africa. Equally he was hurt by the loss of Private Martin in Italy and so many of his colleagues at the ill-fated Arnhem escapade including his dear comrade Alfred Penwill on their drop on Monday 18th September 1944.

I know this first-hand because when he went back to Arnhem for the first time in 1991 (a mere 47 years later than his previous visit) he and I took the opportunity to drive over the new bridge in Arnhem.

When we were on the bridge I asked him how he felt about it and in his typical manner said, "I feel like telling you to stop the car and let me get out and have a piddle over the edge because this bloody bridge caused the loss of so many good men."

It cannot be any clearer than that. He hated losing good men because he saw it as his duty as their Sergeant to take great care of them.

Talking of Penwill and our trip to Holland in 1991, I will always remember his agitation at not being able to find Alf's grave. We first visited the Canadian cemetery at Nijmegen only to find his name on the wall where we left some flowers out of respect.

But at long last, we found his grave at the Oosterbeek cemetery. The relief on my Dad's face was obvious. He could be at rest because he knew his pal finally had a proper resting place and some form of recognition. At least Albert had somewhere to go to pay his respects.

What this story highlights is that these elite men are still human beings and they have feelings as well as principles.

Hopefully the point is made.

I feel pretty sure these highly trained men were not always allowed to perform as they should, frankly, because of the petty politics at the time.

This would have frustrated Albert and have possibly prompted his move to the Paras.

In the meantime he was involved in his totally committed kill or be killed manner.

AND SO IN TO ACTION

He took part in the ill-fated Litani River raid on the Lebanese coast in June 1941. The 11th suffered heavy losses including the death of their Commanding Officer Colonel Richard Pedder in the very early stages.

This was the first time in action for Albert and his comrades. They were a close knit bunch having trained and lived together for several months on Arran as part of this exciting new adventure.

Then the reality of war kicks in and so many of your pals are lost forever.

In Albert's words, this is how he saw it when asked by Hans Vervoorn what he thought of the French. "Well when 500 of us went ashore on the Litani River in 1941 the Vichy French put up the white flags of surrender only for them to take them down once we were up on the high ground and machine gun us. We suffered heavy losses. To be honest Hans, I was never keen on the French from that day forward."

The memory runs deep. This was a matter of life and death; the reality of war. These highly trained men were simply gun fodder. Indeed, Albert was hit but that wasn't going to stop him.

As a family we still have copies of photos of various graves from that time which he sent back home with real telling comments of the loss of his colleagues.

The photos included are not of a particularly good quality however you will see two of them with Albert's handwritten notes on the back. I know it is repetition however, Albert's words tell exactly how it was, they are not for the faint hearted reading;

"All the men on this board are buried in the cemetery under the heading of Unknown Soldiers of the Eleventh Scottish Commando. They were unrecognisable we know where they fell."

"LCpl Cohen, he tried to save Sgt Burton but a sniper got him."

I don't know about you but they certainly pull at the heart strings. They show the raw reality of war!

The other significant raid that he was on was the one to capture Rommel at his headquarters in the Libyan desert, I think, in November 1941.

The bright idea was to capture each other's generals as a means of shortening the war. That is why Montgomery had so many lookalikes.

The Commandos under the leadership of their new Commanding Officer Geoffrey Keyes would go ashore off two submarines at night and make their way to Rommel's desert abode.

Unfortunately, only one of the forces was able to land due to a heavy swell on the Mediterranean Sea. Keyes' cohort got ashore, the other one didn't. Fortunate for the Spring family, Albert and his comrades did not make it.

Off the other force went to complete their mission. As it happened Rommel wasn't there, he wasn't even in Africa as he was in Paris for a long weekend with his wife!

The best laid plans of mice and men!

There was fierce fighting at the villa where, amongst others Keyes was killed in action for which he received a posthumous Victoria Cross. The losses were heavy and indeed only a few of the Commando force made it back alive many months later. If my facts are right one of those was the famous Jack Terry. He and his colleague had been looked after by the Bedouin Arabs.

Albert told me of another such mission when they went ashore on the north African coast to blow up the power station at Bardia.

This time they got off the submarine and into the folbots safely and came ashore, where they formed up and left a comrade to guard the boats.

The main party then set off on the twenty plus miles hike for the targeted power station site.

Not far down the track, they noticed an enemy out rider on a motor bike coming towards them. As per their drill they split half and half each side of the road with both sides throwing hand grenades at the rider and missing and injuring their own men either side of the track.

After that unexpected skirmish they decided to abort the raid because the all important element of surprise had been lost. They sent an Officer back to the look out to make him aware they were coming back.

When the Officer arrived back he had forgotten the password and the lookout shot him!

Remember, these men were not in standard uniform hence the Officer could easily have been the enemy.

To cap it all Albert on his return home on leave saw the banner headline from Churchill's war propaganda machine that read "Crack Allied soldiers destroy enemy power station at Bardia." He laughed and said, "we never got within twenty miles of the damn thing." Alas the follies of war!

There did not appear to be any set pattern to the operations or, maybe knowing Albert, he did not see them as relevant, however, here are a few glimpses of his experiences there.

You may have heard of a submarine called the HMS Thetis or later HMS Thunderbolt which had quite a history all of its own. It was built at the Cammell Laird & Company ship yard on the River Mersey in Birkenhead Liverpool in 1938.

In the rush to get the boats into action the builders decided to take the Thetis to sea for her sea trials early with the full crew and some of her fit out build team still on board to complete the outstanding work at the same time.

The trials took place in May 1939 in Liverpool Bay which is that mass of water bounded by the north Wales coast and the north west coast of England.

Whilst testing the submerging and re-surfacing capabilities of the submarine on that fateful day 1st June 1939 they submerged, and then found it was not possible to bring the vessel back to the surface.

Tragically, the rescue attempts were in vain and, sadly, all those on board perished.

After time, the salvage operation brought the submarine back to the surface, when the daunting task of recovering the bodies and clearing out the debris with a view to refitting and recommissioning the boat ready for service.

If you go to Holyhead, on Anglesey, there is a Naval Club where the submarine and the tragedy are remembered. If I remember correctly some of those lost are buried there.

Many years ago, ironically, I was on a sailing weekend there and we happened to visit the Naval Club for a drink or two and I saw the name Thetis and the penny dropped.

The submarine was recommissioned and renamed HMS Thunderbolt and put into service in the Mediterranean.

Would you believe, Albert told us of working off the Thunderbolt as part of his special forces operations when undertaking the various missions.

One of his particular stories related to how they operated at night. Given the nature of their secret operations there were no lights or talking. Whilst these men were super fit and even better trained, they did have their limits under the most of extreme conditions.

They carried a huge amount of kit, sometimes equating to their own body weight, which meant despite their super skills, they could not manage to swim or even tread water when they were fully loaded up.

So how did they manage to get off the deck of the submarine in to their folbots to go ashore with a view to creating total mayhem?

The answer was they jumped off the side of the sub hoping to land in the canvas boat with a rope tied to their belt and the other end to the rail on the submarine.

This was their safety mechanism just in case they missed which they did on a regular basis.

But how did the crew know if they had missed? It was very simple; if the rope stayed taught for two minutes they knew the individual had missed and was under water whereupon they hoisted them back up to have another go!

This is what made the likes of my dad a bit special. Can you imagine doing just that the once let alone on a regular basis. They were also very strong of mind as well as the body.

When asked by Hans Vervoorn in 1991 if he liked swimming Albert replied, "I was a very good strong swimmer but after the rope staying tight a few times, I can't say I enjoyed it." Now, is that not truly remarkable which sets them aside from others?

Those of you who knew Albert back in Winwick after the war will recall he had a pair of rather special binoculars.

Albert, being Albert, never said much about them. Although it has been said they were actually the night glasses of a German soldier and it was suggested Albert may have shot him to get his prize. At the end of the day war is war!

Sadly, those glasses, which Albert must have had for the best part of fifty years, were removed from his car when he had to leave it after an accident down Huntingdon way.

Whoever finished up with them, I sincerely hope they appreciate the history they are handling and the stories they could tell!

Albert would have used them when out at night looking after his beloved rearing pheasants. Given they were night sight glasses he will have tracked many a predator such as a fox with them. Even in the pitch black of night it would look like a bright day.

They didn't have the benefit of the technology we have today but they could certainly navigate and find their targets wherever they went.

NORTH AFRICA WITH THE LRDG & THE SAS

In his time with the Long Range Desert Group (LRDG) there were many adventures but not all of the happy kind.

The LRDG was a combined force of these renegades who could live and thrive in the harsh environment of a vast desert. If my geography serves me right there are none larger than the deserts of North Africa.

They were a motley but deadly crew made up of a mixture of Commandos and the SAS types who would certainly struggle to fit in with standard expectations of the normal soldier.

That was what made them so special. They could take on the most outrageous of tasks, complete them successfully and then disappear into the desert night as they did on so many occasions.

They simply roamed those Northern African deserts, hiding by day and blowing up Rommel's aircraft and bases by night.

To give you an idea of their capability, the records show that Paddy Mayne himself destroyed over one hundred enemy aircraft with his own bare hands plus no doubt supported by a Bren Gun or two with a few hand grenades here and there.

They worked up to three hundred miles deep into the desert behind enemy lines.

Albert described the desert as like a gigantic ocean with the sand ridges being akin to huge waves. Many a time they would be aware that another patrol, most likely German, travelling parallel to them on the other side of a huge wave of sand.

I understand from Steven Pressfield's book "Killing Rommel" all the forces looked and dressed alike, indeed sometimes they travelled together because it was sometimes safer that way. It was a question of timing; get it right and fine, they were on their way. Get it wrong and you could be in real trouble.

Equipment wise, these fighting nomads had very little; obviously they had the trucks armed with the mounted machine guns and the like. They had hand guns and grenades and that was about it.

They also had the stars, the sun and good basic compasses to navigate their way over vast areas that all looked the same. The only issue was when the sun was directly overhead, particularly through the middle of the day, they couldn't navigate any way.

Therefore, the modus operandi was simple; at night travel, destroy your objective and disappear. By day they made camp by circling their trucks and covering them with huge camouflage nets.

So fight by night and rest by day.

Albert said, with a grin, when they were laying up by day the only people whoever shot at them were the British!

This is Boys Own stuff but with deadly consequences. You were constantly on your guard because you could be ambushed at any time.

The regular routine was to blow up the aircraft, destroy the facilities and kill as many of the enemy as possible. And then simply disappear into thin air!

In reading Steven Pressfield's book, I found myself thinking Albert would have enjoyed this adventure where you are battling adversity to achieve your objectives.

Remember, the Axis forces were winning the war in North Africa, which was pivotal to who the eventual winners would be.

There were large numbers of service men and equipment in that vast desert morass but the fighting was going nowhere.

Could it be, these renegades held the key in breaking this all important deadlock? Rommel was very clever and astute, who anyone worth their salt, considered to be truly remarkable man. Indeed a truly worthy foe.

Defeating him was absolutely crucial. When you see how it was portrayed in the SAS Rogue Heroes series of TV programmes this non-descript band of brothers held the key.

The analogy in sporting terms is the deadlock between two mighty and able teams is, invariably, broken by an unexpected stroke of genius or at least a stroke of brilliance delivered by a force that is not considered normal.

That is what made these people truly remarkable. This motley dishevelled bunch held the key to the most important prize in our modern history.

Can you imagine how proud we are of Albert, our dad, and the part he played in it. We simply bristle with pride at the very thought. For him this wasn't going for a walk up Hamerton Grove or doing a bit of poaching on a windy Saturday evening back home. This was real life and death.

Albert said he worked with David Stirling who became the first Commanding Officer of the SAS or the L Detachment as they were quaintly called. Stirling was a renegade, as wild as the wind but he wasn't known as the Phantom Major for nothing. In checking Albert's army service records again he must have worked with Stirling when he was in 1SAS in late 1942 early 1943 or when the 11th were part of the Middle East Commando!

The more your research the more you realise there were so many and varied types of special forces such as the Layforce and Middle Eastern Commando (MEC) hence I find it difficult to be too accurate as to what really when on.

No wonder Adolf Hitler made them the Axis' forces number one enemy in the North Africa theatre of war!

This reminds me of Albert attending the 50th anniversary of the Battle of Arnhem in 1994. One of the organised events involved attending a large function led by John 'Shan' Hackett who had been a senior Officer there back in 1944. Father shook Sir John's hand and they chatted. He asked Albert how he was and then they talked about their time in Africa and the Middle East. Clearly they had met long before Arnhem in totally different circumstances.

Hackett was infact an Australian who could speak eight different languages including Arabic. He was a remarkable man.

Look him up. His book "I was a Stranger" tells of his remarkable escape from Arnhem after he was badly injured. The Dutch people, at great risk to themselves and their families, had hidden him for several months before his escape.

Witnessing their reunion some fifty plus years later demonstrated the special bond between these remarkable people.

Albert would never let anyone down; his word and deed was his bond. It was as simple as that. From our viewpoint, he was perfect for these unique circumstances. He would never let anyone down, no matter the cost.

No wonder Hitler dreaded such people who could attack his mighty forces and then simply disappear in to thin air, other than it wasn't fresh air, it was extremely hot with temperatures of 30 to 40 degrees centigrade common place by day and then down to near freezing at night without the power of the sun.

That is one hell of a diurnal range.

As with the Commandos the records are not clear. Therefore we are unsure exactly what Albert got up to there.

My brother Dan has reminded me of another little story about soldier fellowship particularly between the Scots and the English when Albert was based north of the Border.

The story goes like this, a particular Scot with a reputation for his tightness at the bar, had a phobia that his comrades would drink his beer whilst he was in the lavatory as they were known in those days; hence he would spit in his pint before going to little boys room.

His mates, or so called, including Albert, in turn would then duly pee in it! When he came back he was none the wiser. Wouldn't it have been easier to take his pint with him?

Dan also said Vine Cottage had a tiled roof and rather than the thatched one I may have suggested earlier.

Likewise the big tree in Granny's orchard was a walnut and not an oak. Danny tells me there were only three oak trees in the parish of Winwick or so father said!

Good job Dan is here to keep me on the straight and narrow!

Talking of the rather basic equipment available to them, Albert, (I do keep wanting to call him father), told me an interesting story from way back then.

He did not say too much and you certainly would not call him a braggart. However, he did casually mention one day that whilst he had been on observation assignments presumably in Middle East / North Africa where they used odd looking microphones that fitted on the external part of the throat area, which meant he only had to mime the words and it transmitted the message to whoever. Remember this is over eighty years ago. How is that for technology in the desert!

Supposedly, it was the demands of the war that brought on such advances in technology.

Interestingly there is a good little book called Secret Britain which tells stories of the various parts of our beloved country the government sequestrated for the war effort where all sorts of weird experiments were conducted with a view to getting one up on the enemy. If I remember correctly, some of those areas have only more recently been declassified and returned to public access.

This all goes to show that, when the pressure is on, we perform at our best in adversity.

On the theme of equipment, reminds me of another example of the propaganda war where the soldiers were addressed by a very high ranking Officer in North Africa. His very strong message was clear; "We are going to win the war because God is on our side." He went on "and how do we know God is on our side? We know because he has given us the biggest and best guns!" Not sure a really experienced (or should I say cynical) soldier of the ilk of Albert was going to fall for that. That is one thing you could always say of him; he certainly kept his feet on the ground!

Having lost so many good mates who can blame him!

Writing this does strange things to my memory inasmuch another memory has come back to mind.

Many years ago I was in the Post Office come shop in the next village of Old Weston on the Cambridgeshire / Northamptonshire border with Albert where he said to a gentleman "these people won't believe what you and I were doing in the North African desert in the war? We were frying eggs on a shovel just with heat of the sun."

Again, what an experience for two country boys all those miles away from home and there must be so many tales like that to be told. Whilst war is not a good thing and certainly not to be condoned by any means; it does allow supposedly ordinary people to share such unique experiences. You could live forever in a Cambridgeshire village and no way would you be able to fry an egg on a shovel just using the heat of the sun!

Albert also had a fringe, but interesting, involvement with Crete or at least it's fall in May / June 1941. He spoke of being mustered to join and set sail on the HMS Kelly commanded by Louis Mountbatten to sail to Crete. However they were advised to turn back because this important island location had fallen to the enemy.

The timing is intriguing because I was of the view that the first action the 11th saw was on the Litani River in June 1941 but they had been called to arms about a month earlier for Crete, albeit in vain.

So there, the country boy got to meet royalty or at least as near to it as he would get at that time. Although he did come across one or more members of the Royal Family later on in his life in the shooting fields.

Mentioning Popski's Army

Again, in casual conversation, Albert mentioned working with a gentleman by the name of Popski in his time with the Commandos and the various escapades in North Africa.

You can look him up; he is famous for making up another specialist forces group roaming the desert regions of the African continent.

The operations of the thousands of soldiers like Albert were rather vague and not always clear. Nonetheless why did he mention the fact he knew and had been involved with Popski. Knowing him, as well as any son knows his father, I must say he must have worked closely with him, and if so what were they doing together in the western desert?

As I said before, how did that work in reality? Having read about Popski and some of his men, it becomes clear that a lot of them became rather addicted to fighting, albeit they were part of the British army, because fighting is a simple but rather risky way of earning a living and perhaps realising their own self-worth in the strangest of environments.

A number of them could not stop because fighting had become their profession and indeed their obsession. I recall reading about one of Popski's right hand men extending his war mongering career in to the heart of Africa after the war and being killed in the late 1950s. Indeed he was another victim of the World War.

For some reason Popski makes me think of private armies. I suspect such so called private armies and possibly mercenary activity has continued through the ages of time to include the more recent times in Iraq, Afghanistan and even right now in the Ukraine.

Wikipedia describes Popski and his army thus

"Popski's Private Army (PPA), officially No. 1 Demolition Squadron, PPA, was a unit of British Special Forces set up in Cairo in October 1942 by Major Vladimir Peniakof (Popski). Popski's private army was one of several raiding units formed in the Western Desert during the Second World War. The squadron also served in Italy and was disbanded in September 1945.

No. 1 Demolition Squadron was formed specifically to attack Field Marshall Rommel's fuel supplies, in support of General Montgomery's offensive at El Alamein, at the suggestion of Lieutenant-Colonel John Hackett. The unit became operational on 10 December 1942 as an 8th Army Special Forces unit. After the Long Range Desert Group (LRDG) and the Special Air Services (SAS), PPA was the last and smallest of the three main irregular raiding, reconnaissance, and intelligence units formed during the North African Campaign."

From what he said Albert found Popski to be a really good operator who he admired and would have loved his no nonsense daring action filled approach.

Can you imagine spending your days, weeks and indeed years roaming the desert in very uncomfortable conditions fighting but perhaps more importantly observing and disrupting the enemy at every turn? What an adventure, albeit very risky, as this whole war business was.

"Killing Rommel" By Steven Pressfield

As I mentioned earlier, spotting this particular book on the shelf of the Waterstones book shop in Macclesfield struck a chord.

From my perspective it is a mixture of fact and fiction but for me appears to be a good reflection of what went on in those heady days where victory in North Africa was mission critical.

There are a number of abiding memories from the book.

The first one being how much Albert would have enjoyed this adventure. He would have relished the challenges it brought of trying do the business in the most unlikely and extreme of circumstances such as, using vehicles not meant for such sandy terrains to achieve their objectives.

Secondly, strange things happen in war and Steven tells the story of one of the LRDG patrols being concerned by several unidentified vehicles appearing to be shadowing them. They waited until sunset and decided to attack just in case.

The story tells of how they opened fire on these vehicles and killed everyone on board. If I remember the quote correctly it went "we didn't just kill them, we turned them into pulp."

As it turned out afterwards, the suspected enemy were a unit of very young raw Italian recruits who represented no harm to such seasoned and hardened soldiers.

This incident, true or otherwise, sums up this dreadful war. It was a vicious business because it was all about killing or, as Albert put it, "kill or be killed." There were no half measures; it simply had to be done and strange things happened.

As a divergence, and talking of strange behaviour, this reminds me of the story of Corporal McLaughlin, a young Para from Liverpool, who was killed in the Falklands War in 1982. His bravery was no doubt and he was nominated for a posthumous Victoria Cross only for it to be denied because when his body was recovered they found a number of Argentinians soldiers ears in his possession.

In speaking to father I said "what a strange thing for anyone to do." His reply was very telling; he said simply "let me tell you, very strange and inexplicable things happen in the heat of battle." And we left it at that!

I wonder what incidents that brief discussion stirred up in the murky depths of his memory from all those years ago!

Up to the point of reading Steven's book I knew Paddy Mayne as a tremendous character that Albert spoke of in a light hearted and rather jovial way. Then, when I got to page 80 something I learnt about the real exploits of this remarkable man and I was blown away. Now I knew what they meant about "walking amongst giants." He was a colossus of a man who truly led from the front. No wonder father respected and admired him so much.

And the final abiding memory being how haphazard it all was. These units were completely on their own. Even their fellow allies stole each other's fuel and essential supplies. The Allies and the Axis troops behaved in exactly the same way. They joined each other's convoys when it suited and was considered a safer way to travel.

Clearly this was no ordinary warfare.

What must have such conditions, such circumstances, memories and such horrific incidents have done to their minds. Perhaps it explains a lot and no wonder all Albert really wanted to do was get back to a peaceful life in the countryside of Winwick and Hamerton

In more recent times I have come across a very interesting Facebook group call "Middle East Commando" (MEC) run by Alan

Orton and Phil Williams. I have found their postings very interesting which has thrown up the odd photograph of Albert from those days. I did not realise there was such a group but clearly their activities were just what he had been involved with in his three years or so with 11th (Scottish) Commando, the Layforce, the MEC, SAS and the LRDG. I cannot thank Alan, Phil and their colleagues for their wonderful skills and depth of knowledge from over eighty years ago.

Such specialist groups are invaluable because they still come up with gems after all this time. As an example, in early 2023, there popped up this post with a photo of a mixed group (forgive me, I nearly called them a rag bag bunch!) of members of the MEC somewhere in North Africa, and there amongst them was Albert kneeling down as only he could. I cannot tell you how proud I felt of this so called ordinary man. More importantly, he was an equal, which tells me he was one of the giants of this time and place or at least in my mind!

The problem with it all is the records are very sketchy and I understand the Commandos and similar units were rather poor with their record keeping. They are there to get on with the action rather than maintaining exemplary records. Perhaps this is another difference with the regular army.

It is also important to mention the assistance received from John Valenti of the United States who, to me, was a fountain of knowledge about the LRDG in those times. Sadly we lost John recently. Deepest condolences to his family.

For the record Albert's army records show that Albert served in 1SAS from November 1942 to January 1943.

I will try to leave those marauding days behind but please forgive me if I drift back there from time to time!

Paddy Mayne & Colleagues

Amongst the ranks of the 11th were some very strong characters including the likes of Paddy Mayne who has recently featured in the recent TV programme "SAS Rogue Heroes" and in Steven Pressfield's book "Killing Rommel" as mentioned earlier.

Newtonards is a small town in the east of Northern Ireland where there is a statue of their local hero, the great Paddy Mayne, who served in the 11th (Scottish) Commando, the Layforce and then on to the SAS operating initially in the Middle East and North Africa and then in many other theatres of war. He took command of the SAS in 1943 when David Stirling was captured.

I am very proud to report I have been there to pay my respects to this great man. If my dad liked and admired him then that is good enough for me. Paddy is a true legend who maybe gone but certainly not forgotten.

Paddy was and still is a remarkable character and personality to many. He is one of the most decorated soldiers of WWII. It is also fair to say he was not everybody's cup of tea.

The reason Paddy joined the SAS was rather bizarre, it was because he had that huge fall out with Geoffrey Keyes in the Middle East. I may be totally wrong, but as I understand it they fell out over a game of chess in the Officers mess with, allegedly, Paddy thumping Geoffrey and, as a result, finishing up on a charge and not wanted back because of his so called bizarre behaviour.

He was a Marmite character who railed against authority which made him ideal for the likes of the specialist forces such as the SAS. On reflection, Paddy Mayne always reminds me of that wonderful quote from the film "Butch Cassidy & the Sundance Kid" when one of them found themselves in a one to one fight against a giant of a man whereupon the smaller man kicked the larger man in the privates. The giant complained "what about the rules?" to which Butch or Sundance responded, "what rules?."

To me, from watching SAS Rogue Heroes and reading many a book about the Commandos, the Long Range Desert Group (LRDG) and the SAS that quote "what rules?" seems to fit well.

Coming back to Albert, and to conclude this particular section on Paddy Mayne. Albert really liked him as they obviously struck a chord with each other. Again, I cannot verify this particular story, however, it goes like this. When Albert and Paddy were working together in the North African desert, knowing of Albert's ability as a poacher to catch any wildlife anywhere Paddy approached Albert about serving up something interesting for the Officers to eat that evening.

Albert went off into the desert only to return with a desert fox which he had shot, Paddy thought this was ideal and concluded the matter by saying " Albert that is fine, you skin and gut it and we will call it jugged hare." As I say I cannot verify this story because I wasn't there and the two protagonists are long gone, but what a fabulous story which epitomises the bond between these remarkable people in even more remarkable and truly bizarre circumstances.

Paddy Mayne struggled to come to terms with the return to so called 'normal' life after his tumultuous and heroic achievements with the Commandos and then the Special Air Service seeing action across numerous continents. He was one of our most decorated soldier of this World War. Sadly and ironically he was killed in 1955 in a car accident just 300 yards from his family home in Newtownards, Northern Ireland at the mere age of 40. What a waste.

Other larger than life characters included Tommy McPherson, who went on to have an illustrious career with the SAS, Jim Storie and Jack Terry, similar, along with Geoffrey Keyes who went on to command the 11th after the untimely death of the original Commanding Officer Richard Pedder.

Another character in the 11th was Paddy's big pal, also from Northern Ireland, Eoin McGonigal. They joined the 11th at the same time in 1940 and went on to serve together in the SAS. Sadly, if I recall correctly, McGonigal was killed when parachuting in to action in high winds whereupon he was blown against rocks and sadly perished without a bullet being fired in anger.

This was back in the days when the strategy for delivering the SAS in to action was by parachute. Many highly trained soldiers were lost due to the high winds encountered particularly in the North African desert of Libya and Egypt.

Another irony that comes to mind, is the fact that our house at 1 Thurning Road, Winwick was on the flight path of the United States Air Force fighter planes at what was RAF Alconbury in Cambridgeshire.

Those of you who can recall the issues with Colonel Gaddafi in the 1970s / 80s when the United States decided to bomb Libya and, you will not believe it, one of the bases used for those attacks was none other than Alconbury. So those fighter jets would have flown over Albert's house having just returned from the same desert areas he had patrolled all those decades earlier.

Isn't that an amazing coincidence?

Believe it or not, I can still hear the extremely loud screech of those F16 jets that shook our house and the very beds we were lying in. It was not just us; it was all six of the houses in our row and the rest of the village.

Thankfully, those days of the USAF at RAF Alconbury are long gone and now redeveloped and Winwick has returned to its rightful slumber!

Albert had been made up to the rank of Sergeant when he was with the Commandos in the Middle East, the exact circumstances of which are vague. I suspect he got his promotion this time for much more than killing rabbits with a stick!

He served as a Sergeant in all his time with the 10th and whilst he was clearly a strict disciplinarian who did not suffer fools gladly, he was not a shouter; he had that air of assured quiet confidence about him. He was that sort of person you would definitely want on your side, that is for sure!

There is a rather thick volume entitled 'The Tenth' which chronicles all about the 10th Battalion The Parachute Regiment and all those who served in it from its inception in 1942 to after Arnhem in 1944, when it was disbanded. Strangely Albert is not mentioned in it. How can that be?

Arthur, our second eldest brother, had this theory which went like this. As you know Hitler decreed that all Commandos were to be shot on sight without any questions asked because he saw them as a total menace who clearly got under his skin big time! Hence, Arthur's theory was Albert was not mentioned in that chronicle because he had been a Commando hence they did not want to name him. Farfetched or what?

Talking of Hitler's edict against the Commandos, I was lucky enough to meet a man, who I was walking with in the Lake District a few years ago, who's uncle had also been one of the Commandos that took part in Operation Musketoon in September 1942, whereupon about a dozen Commandos went ashore by submarine on the north west coast of Norway to blow up a hydroelectric power plant at Glomfjord, near the artic circle.

Supported by a few of the Norwegian special resistance forces they were successful in their mission. However, one of the German guards noticed a fresh cigarette butt and put his comrades on alert resulting in a search which discovered the perpetrators.

It is not clear what happened to the Norwegians, but history tells exactly what happened to the British Commandos. They were some of the very first to be dealt with under Hitler's edict. Hence they were taken to Colditz Castle and executed with a bullet through the head.

To conclude this particular story those very brave mens' instructions were; you are on your own; blow up the plant and make your way to Sweden, which of course was neutral hence was considered a safe haven. Only if they had the chance to get that far. Operation Musketoon was a fine example of a truly clandestine operation.

On a similar theme, I have always wanted to visit the Lofoten Islands at the top of Norway to see where another of the early Commando raids took place in World War II in order to protect the area from the Russians and the Germans.

Very brave and remarkable achievements by any standard. You can imagine our pride at our father being amongst them. Don't you think "No Ordinary Man" about sums Albert up?

JOINING THE 10ᵀᴴ BATTALION THE PARACHUTE REGIMENT

Whilst the details are sketchy of how it all happened, Albert took the next step in his army career changing from one special force to another when he transferred to the 10th Battalion The Parachute Regiment, according to his army records, in early 1943.

As mentioned earlier, it may have been the shilling a day danger money that did it, or simply the frustration of the Commandos not getting the support they needed or it was time to move on to a new challenge?

Albert was still in Egypt undertaking his Parachute training at Kabrit, which, ironically, was constructed as a parachute training centre for the Commandos and the SAS.

They got up to all sorts of antics as part of the training process such as rolling out of the back of speeding trucks to learn how to roll when they landed. No wonder they gave them danger money!

Likewise, they jumped from gantries at differing heights to learn how to land properly, without doing too much harm to themselves.

As they practised their technique improved so the better they got it became time to graduate to the real thing of jumping out of an actual aircraft.

In total Albert did 38 operational jumps. I am not sure how an operational jump is defined. Presumably, it means action jumps against the enemy or in operations against the enemy.

It was interesting listening to Albert and Jim Westbury, who was one of Albert's right hand men.

They spoke of how they did their jumps earlier in the morning because the Egyptian heat created problems with thermals. This meant the parachutes and indeed the attached Parachutist could be found hovering some one to two hundred feet above the ground if they got caught in one such thermal.

This wasn't a regular occurrence. However, if it did happen the other more fortunate Paras who landed fairly and squarely on the ground would shout up to their comrades "if you are still there when we have finished our breakfast we will get you down." So how did they do it? it was rather simple really. The soldiers on the ground would fire a machine gun to shoot out the middle of the chute to release the pocket of trapped warm air out through the newly formed hole until such time the Para hit the ground. Then they too could go and have their belated breakfast!

Albert being the country boy he was, soon made friends with a terrier dog by the name of Bill, who used to join Albert and his mates in the aircraft and always wanted to jump out with him. So no more to do, Albert made him a parachute of his very own, so he could be seen parachuting down to the ground alongside his master!

Now there is a surprise.

Another amusing anecdote involved two of the Paras being in the medical orderly's waiting room amongst a few of their comrades.

After one of their particular comrades had been seen and had left, one said to the other "did you see that, was it real or am I imaging things?"

They had both witnessed one of their fellow Paras, who had a bullet wound one side of his head with a ridge of skin that went all the way over his head with another bullet exit wound on the other side.

Yes, this particular soldier had been lucky enough to be hit by a bullet which for some very fortunate reason had been deflected under his scalp and right over his head, avoiding his delicate brain area, and came out the other side.

How lucky is that?

Not in Kabrit, but another story of when father was in hospital in Winwick just north of Warrington, in what must have been Lancashire then.

What a coincidence to finish up in hospital in Winwick Lancashire when you come from Winwick in Huntingdonshire!

It was no ordinary hospital; it was indeed a mental hospital which had been sequestrated for the military and still used for its civilian patients.

I assumed Albert was in there because he had injured his back somewhere parachuting maybe even at Ringway which was a major training base for Airborne Army troops as they were known. Albert did tend to suffer from a bad back and Dan puts that down to when he landed on a gate post on one of his many drops.

Dan tells me my assumption was incorrect because father was in there because of a war time trauma in North Africa when he had witnessed a number of his comrades burning to death after the explosion of a fuel tanker in the desert after a surprise enemy attack. Dan recalled a conversation whereby father made the comment "when people burn to death they appear to come alive and move in front of you." Nothing more was said until Dan asked mother a few days later what was meant by Albert's comment.

Mother explained the incident by saying Albert had been traumatised when he and his colleagues had encountered a surprise attack whilst in the desert and they dived under their two vehicles for shelter. One of the trucks was a normal lorry with the other one being a fuel tanker. As per chance Albert had dived under the normal lorry and then saw the fuel tanker go up in flames hence his reference to watching people burn to death.

As a result, he needed psychiatric treatment hence his stay in Winwick Hospital. Every mind has its limits even if you are a super fit highly trained soldier.

One lunch time Albert and one of the Officers were walking down the hospital corridor on their way to lunch when one of the asylum patients, who had his ear to the wall, beckons them over and says to them "can you hear what I can hear?" They duly took it in turns to have a listen.

They looked at each other rather puzzled and then turned and said, "we didn't hear a thing" to which the patient replies, "neither did I!"

Now which of them had the mental issue?

As background, the formation of the 10th Battalion was led by Colonel Kenneth Smyth OBE of the Royal Sussex Regiment, which meant there was a predominance of Officers from that particular Regiment as the mother Regiment.

Therefore, the rush was on to recruit the men for the non-commissioned ranks, especially given the Battalion was being formed overseas. Dare I say, Egypt was like a transit camp for all sorts of so called military waifs and strays. That sounds harsh because a lot of them were highly trained and very fit men who were looking for a new direction.

Having spoken to a number of Commando veterans, some of them did not relish jumping out of an aircraft. They would rather yomp 250 miles across the desert rather than jump out of an aeroplane!

Therefore, given Paratroopers were the new kids on the block, a lot of them saw themselves as the ultimate elite force.

Such a mindset caused issues of arrogance and dis-obedience. As Albert was a strong disciplinarian, I am convinced he was encouraged to join the Paras because they desperately needed his sort of discipline as they could be an unruly bunch!

This leads on to what Jim Westbury told me. He and a number of his mates, such as Reg Shurbourne, were from the Kings Own Yorkshire Light Infantry (KOYLI).

He said, "do you know the first words your dad ever said to me?" I said "no" to which he replied, "Westbury you might break the girls hearts but you won't break mine."

To give you another example, they were joking one day of an incident when they were on parade either in Kabrit or Palestine on a very hot day.

The troops were being inspected by Regimental Sergeant Major (RSM) White and he was walking behind Jim, Reg and others when the RSM said "boy am I hurting you?" The answer was "no sir." To which the response was "well I ought to be as I am standing on your hair."

They were immediately dismissed to get their hairs cut. Upon their return with extremely short haircuts they were put on a charge for insubordination!

That is how it could be when certain Regiments were labelled as special or indeed even elite.

As a further example of the same, I made the acquaintance of Jim Longson from Whaley Bridge near Buxton. Jim was a Staffordshire Regiment man who went in to Arnhem by glider. Jim made it clear he hated the Paras, going straight to the point, he called them "bloody glory boys in their fancy red berets." No love lost there then!

All of which reinforces my argument that discipline was much needed!

A particular incident at Ringway Airport in the early days of the Airborne Army, as they were known in their infancy, reinforced the need for strong leadership and discipline.

Given that, like with the Commandos, Churchill was a strong supporter of such specialist highly trained soldiers who could be delivered from the air by parachute for a surprise attack that would totally unnerve the enemy. This was all about that element of surprise in tactical warfare using a smaller group of fleet of foot forces, rather than the slower more traditional forces, which deeply troubled the Fuhrer and his henchmen.

And what is more, the Germans had Paratroopers already and were using them to great effect. Churchill was not to be outdone by the enemy!

As a result, a group of men were assembled at Ringway to be trained to be Paratroopers with drops into the nearby rather large Tatton Park. If you were unlucky, you could finish up dropping in the lake which was not much fun.

In those early days, the parachutes could be unreliable and occasionally malfunctioned, presumably because of the haste of their procurement and manufacture.

As a coincidence in Macclesfield where I live there is a well-known furniture store by the wonderful name of Arighi Bianchi who undertook the manufacture of parachutes in World War II. Maybe they supplied them to Ringway. I can recall Paul Bianchi and his son Nick telling how they employed ladies to make the silk parachutes back then.

There was one such incident whereby one of the recruits' parachute did not open and sadly he fell to his death in the very same park. Just think about the guy who was immediately behind him who saw his pal fall to his death. How unnerving would that have been?

The obvious reaction would be hesitation or total refusal at worst. The instructors were having none of that so immediately kicked the next guy out. His chute, thankfully, opened and he landed safely. No doubt this was not an isolated incident.

The decisive action by those instructors meant the next in line did not have time to refuse.

The assembled throng fancied themselves as the bee's knees and the best of the best. With that came the arrogance of a so called elite group.

So much so that the concern felt regarding the situation got as far as Winston Churchill who, acted decisively by sending one of his senior officials to talk to this group of his pet forces.

The said official mounted the platform to address the men and started to speak. At which time he was immediately shouted down by the recruits and promptly made a hasty retreat back to London for his own good.

Discipline was always an issue with these fighting men and hence this is where people like Albert came into their own because they stood no nonsense.

Another example of such belligerence involved Jim Westbury. There was an inspection of the troops somewhere in the Palestine / Egypt area by a high ranking Officer.

As he went along the ranks he inevitably came to Jim, all smartly turned out with his medals gleaming. As the Officer stopped at Jim he remarked "well boy, you have a lot of medals, what did you get them for?" Jim quickly and curtly replied "Fighting Sir." The conversation continued whereby the Officer said, "you have more medals than me boy, why is that so?" Jim with his strong wit responded, "Perhaps I have done more fighting than you Sir." The Officer was heard to say, "you insolent bastard." before he moved on.

That epitomised the attitude of these men; they were arrogant as they believed they were superior to the rest. They were not liked by their fellow Regiments infact maybe that is putting it mildly.

Moving on, Albert spoke of his time in early 1943 when they were based in Ramat David, near Nazareth in Palestine as it was then before the formation of the state of Israel.

From those discussions, I got the impression they were more of a peace keeping force with some form of brief to protect the Jews who were assembling there even in 1943 in their so called 'Promised Land.'

He spoke of toiling in the hot sun erecting huge protective fenced enclosures to protect the Jews from the Palestinians overnight at least.

He then said they would leave the Jews safely ensconced within their protected enclosure of an evening only to discover the next morning they had burrowed underneath and tunnelled their way out!

Albert's simple summary was "you could tell there was going to be trouble and we were best out of it." How prophetic were his words in one of the hotbeds of the world which remains an issue today over eighty years later.

As I write this I have a tingling feeling at the very thought that our father played his own very small part in history at the birth of the new home for the Jews.

It ranks alongside marching through Cape Town and his escapades with the Commandos, the Layforce, 1SAS, the LRDG and the Middle East Commando all those thousands of miles from his true home of little old Winwick.

In thinking about it, Albert saw action in two or three of the hot spots in the Middle East and North Africa regions, namely the Lebanon, Palestine / Israel and stretching the geography a little,

Libya. There was no gentle introduction for him and his comrades; it was in at the deep end, literally, in three of the most sensitive parts of the world that have seen their fair share of trouble and turmoil since then.

Coming back to his time as a Para, not so much is really known of what else the 10th got up to in Palestine / North Africa.

We do know they took part in the invasion of Italy in 1943. Before that, let me tell you another of Albert's stories which does not seem to be too logical of his time there with the 10th.

He told me the story of a rather strange event when both the British and the German Paratroopers dropped on the same drop zone at the same time one evening.

He gave the impression that he was one of those British Paras because he said both parties' Paras were next to and intermingled with each other on the ground at the same time. It was not open warfare or chaos; apparently it was quite civilised. He said when they were collecting the respective containers they often found a British soldier at one end and a German at the other. How did he know they were German, well that was easy he explained because you could smell them!

So what did they do? They just rolled away until they found somebody on their side and when they were ready they formed up ready to move away.

He said their objective was to take a bridge somewhere on, I am sure he said, Sicily. On this occasion the British were quicker off the mark in forming up and moving off in search of their objective. This matched the normal pattern of engagement because the German Paratroopers were much more deliberate and slower in their operations, hence, it was known they would regroup and attack the next morning so the British needed to be ready.

I remember this story in particular because when the British got to the bridge it was dark and the Italians had retired to their beds, hence, the British had to wake them to take them prisoner and no shots were fired in anger!

The other key point was the slight guilty feeling Albert expressed because some bright spark had the idea of taking the Germans by surprise the next morning by swapping uniforms with the Italians. So when the Germans duly approached they were waving to their allies only to find they weren't what they pretended to be.

He said, "we let them have it with heavy fire, they simply didn't stand a chance." He said they felt so bad they ceased fire to help the wounded enemy and then opened fire again to complete the job.

The bridge was successfully taken, although, the victors had reservations about the way they had achieved their objective.

As I say Albert showed a little contrition that day, but after all it was war.

My conundrum is, as I hinted before, there is no record of 10 Para having been engaged in Sicily because the missions there were undertaken by other Para Battalions. Was he and his fellow Paras seconded to them or am I imagining things in my old age? Hopefully not!

ITALY HERE WE COME

So it is goodbye to the heat of the Middle East as the War is progressing well for the Allies in Italy in 1943. They have the upper hand, and it is time for a mopping up operation, particularly in the south.

Therefore, the 10th are used for just that purpose but this time not delivered by a parachute drop but going ashore by boat in the inside of the heel of Italy at the Port of Taranto.

The Axis troops had not totally surrendered; hence caution was needed as the next few paragraphs will show.

They set off on foot with the intention of dealing with situations as they arose.

Albert was being cautious because of his strong belief in protecting his men; the 'nations greatest resource' if you remember.

Sadly he lost one of them namely young Private Martin, as Albert called him, who was killed in street fighting in the country town of Castellaneta in Apulia in southern Italy.

Father spoke of the loss of Martin and even after all those years even in to his dotage, he deeply regretted the loss of this young soldier in his charge. Albert would have been twenty seven at this time and was an experienced soldier with the best part of three years of action under his belt. He saw it as his duty as an experienced soldier and non-commissioned Officer to look after the more vulnerable.

This comes back to his mantra as a country person of protecting the weak and vulnerable from the stronger predators.

Likewise, there was another major casualty in this section although it did not affect Albert directly but was a strategic blow when Major General George Frederick Hopkinson was killed on the

9th September 1943 whilst observing the operations in the area of Castellaneta. This was a serious psychological blow to lose such a high ranking Officer in what was considered to be a relatively safe operation. It is not considered good practice to lose such top brass in such circumstances.

There was fierce street fighting in Castellaneta and I recall Albert speaking of Jim Westbury who was a Bren gunner of some renown and, as you know, one of his right hand men. He talked of watching Jim in action firing down this street. Albert swore Jim was at his best in such circumstances. Indeed he said Jim was the first man he called upon when as he put it "the going got sticky!" That is why Albert favoured him!

Jim told me they had taken some Germans prisoner there and instead of them being a burden, Jim and his comrades put them to work carrying ammunition and equipment in return for food and rations. Jim said then one day they simply disappeared and Jim was not happy. Maybe this being a practicality of war.

There is another more amusing incident in this operation where their company came under a surprise attack. The immediate reaction was to dive for cover.

One of them, by the name of Joe Beet, jumped over a wall for safety which turned out to be not as safe as he thought because he had jumped into effectively a compost heap some fifteen feet below the wall!

When the skirmish was over they could not find Joe, but eventually, after a search, they found him behind the said wall up to his neck in stinking compost with his gun held high over his head.

There was plenty of cussing, to be polite about it, and Joe never lived it down.

I have added this story just for Tina Alderman as was and now Tina Rodwell. Joe was Tina's favourite because she learnt of his, and indeed Albert's exploits because, as the daughter of his next door neighbours at 2 Thurning Road Winwick, she would help him extract his honey in the garage.

At the same time as spinning the honey comb Albert would tell Tina of his war time exploits in his unguarded moments. Indeed we suspect he imparted far more to young Tina than to any of us.

Tina is a wonderful human being who is an important member of our team who has been with us back to Arnhem on several occasions.

For the record Tina always referred to Albert as Mr Spring, even to this day over twenty years since he died. The respect between them was mutual because he rarely opened up but he did to young Tina, particularly at honey extraction time!

Having visited Castellaneta myself it is a rather sleepy town of no apparent significance at first glance however upon reflection, strategically it does look down on the lower lying area to the south and this is perhaps the reason why the Germans / Italians put up a fierce resistance there.

The 10th then made relatively good and steady progress going north east through Italy mopping up as they went, and finally arriving in the port of Bari on the Adriatic coast where they enjoyed some Rest and Recreation (R&R) after several months of being on alert and constantly in action.

Not much is said of their time there but there are some interesting snippets.

Albert speaking of his men said it was very important to have an eclectic mix of skills within the company. As he said you need "someone who can pick a lock, some who can get a motor going against all the odds and someone who could go and find exactly what you needed at that all important moment without too many questions asked!"

Such a moment came in their time there. Albert said in their moments of relaxation they were desperate for the taste of sugar in their tea or coffee having been deprived of it for a very long time. So a group of men were sent on this all important mission in, what was effectively, the Aladdin's cave of the docks and all that comes with it!

As an aside, Albert loved his sugar too. I remember him taking four good spoonful's in his tea, perhaps that is where I get my rather sweet tooth!

Those Paras did not disappoint; not only did they find a bag of sugar. I am not talking of a small 2lb or 1kg bag that we find in our shops today; they came back with one whole one hundred weight hessian bag full. Not only did they bring back such a treasured prize but they delivered it on a proper sack barrow to make its transport much easier. There was no point in making the job harder than it really needs to be. If you are going to do a job do it properly!

Word must have got round because Lionel Queripel, who went on to win a posthumous Victoria Cross less than a year later at Arnhem, would make the excuse of an evening to leave the Officers mess to "inspect his men" to partake of a cup of tea or two with plenty of sugar!

Talking of Queripel, it is not a good idea to have such elite fighting forces twiddling their thumbs because as the saying goes 'the devil makes work for idle hands' and indeed minds!

I am not sure where I came across it but I picked up a bit of gossip about the 10th being involved in a bit of mischief whilst in the port of Bari.

The story goes like this; and mind, it is only a story without any substantiation.

It is alleged a brewery was raided in Bari whilst the Paras were there. Now I asked Albert about this and of any potential involvement. The response was a typical stiff upper lip one. "We don't talk about such things".

This was what they were all about, by God could they fight but they also had a great sense of humour mixed with their mischievous activities as well.

They were not daunted by any challenge and went about it in a typically pragmatic improvised British manner. Nobody knew this better than their German foe who gave them the wonderful nickname "The Red Devils". There is no greater honour.

After all, didn't they deserve a bit of fun given what they had been through!

As a footnote, I am so proud to say that I have visited the very spot where they came alongside the quay in the heel of Italy up though Castellaneta to Bari.

It is pretty ordinary countryside for such a beautiful country but it was obviously a strategic geographical area in this time of the war.

Homeward Bound

The job was done therefore it was time for home and a regroup for their next assignment. The 10th Battalion The Parachute Regiment left Italy arriving in Liverpool on the 19th December 1943 just in time for Christmas.

When they arrived they were dispatched to that rural part of Leicestershire, in the area of Somerby and Burrow on the Hill, which would be their physical home for the next nine months or so, and eventually their adopted home for evermore.

After being all those miles from home Albert was now within a good thirty odd mile bike ride from Winwick which he would not think twice about.

He, like all the others, had effectively been away for over two and a half years. It is all a bit sketchy but presumably most of them had not been home on leave in all that time hence it must have been so good to be safely back home given Albert was a married man with the one son Peter.

It must have been even more special given it was Christmas time. I suspect such moments could have been bitter sweet after being away for such a long time and simply coming back and expecting things to be the same as the day they left some two years or so earlier. There are many stories of relationships not standing the test of time which is understandable under the circumstances.

Thankfully, that was not the case here and, indeed, with the benefit of hindsight now Olive gave birth to their second son Arthur on 19th October 1944.

Being away and fighting a war was one thing, but in my book, the true unsung heroes were those who were left behind such as our mum Olive who had the stresses of bringing up the two boys, running a home plus the worry of whether her husband was ever coming back especially given what had happened to Granny Farrer some twenty six years or so earlier.

Likewise, Granny Farrer and so many people like her are so so special to me. These are the people who also deserved the biggest medals ever. My mum and my granny are my super heroes.

We talk of the war heroes and how many medals they have won but where were the medals for those super heroes left back at home?

Talking to Albert about the fighting; he was the complete pragmatist like he was all his life. His view was simple; it had to be done and the further it was from home the better.

But he was no fool; he said he was concerned about the war going on as it was now into its fifth year and again he put it very simply; the longer it went on the greater chance there was of a bullet with his name on it. In modern parlance, and in a perverse way, it was like doing the lottery. The more you play the better chance of winning, albeit it was losing in this case! Hope that makes sense.

Understandably, he was keen to see the end of the war because, whoever won, it was going to be the millions of fighting families that lost. This is where I get on my soap box about war being futile but, as before, Albert said it is inevitable where there are human beings. And as he agreed with Churchill 'jaw jaw is better than war war' to which Albert added "the only problem is you have to have the 'war war' before the 'jaw jaw'!

That is why it breaks my heart to see all those graves from the two great wars. It is the common man who pays the price with their lives. It is never those who cause these catastrophic events. It makes my blood boil.

THEIR SOMERBY HOME

After Christmas, it was back to training at their new home. Rural Leicestershire was much more normal to these Anglophiles than the heat of desert, Palestine and the Mediterranean.

Albert would have loved being back home so to speak as he was back amongst his treasured countryside. He was back amongst the villages of Somerby and Burrow on the Hill, and it would have been right up his street. He would have loved getting back to his old lifetime ways and habits such as catching rabbits or shooting pheasants.

There is a story that just before they went to Arnhem that September day father had caught five rabbits in the snares he routinely set. He subsequently gutted and legged them and left them hanging on the village butchers door handle with a note that read 'gone away for a few days but will be back for my money.' How is that for self-confidence? If only he had known!

This was Albert very much back where he belonged and he would have felt most confident. He could keep an eye on his family including his much loved mum. There was always a very special bond between them forged out of those very testing years going back to those dreadful times of the First World War.

It didn't mean he spent lavish amounts of money on her because he simply did not have that luxury. It was more important than that; it was the simple things of being with her and just checking up on her. How I wish I had talked to my Granny about how she felt about those times, although, I suspect I would have got the typical British stiff upper lip response.

Coming back to his army life, I suspect there was a hint of frustration at the lack of action as there was during all that time training on the Isle of Arran.

If nothing else, Albert was a man of action. He would be an extremely frustrated man in this modern world where we talk and talk about the easiest of things when it is far quicker to just go and do it!

He spoke of there being many missions where these super men Paratroopers were going into action to hopefully play their part in bringing this damn war to an end. They got geared up and then they were stood down at the last minute. I can imagine he would have been so frustrated.

I can recall him saying he thought the same was going to happen with Operation Market Garden; to take the three bridges at Eindhoven, Nijmegen and finally Arnhem; the Bridge Too Far.

They were expecting it to be cancelled but, it wasn't. The records show the final details were put together in about a week, as a result of which there were many mistakes made or should I say a lack of planning down to the final crucial details that mattered.

When I suggested to Albert that those Officers responsible for planning and executing this particular operation had a lot to answer for he bit my head off with the curt response of "do not criticise our Officers as they were the best and they led from the front."

He and so many of his comrades took to the village life so well, indeed, they were at home. There were a few funny stories.

His respect and admiration for Lionel Queripel ran deep. He did not bother with reveille in the morning, he had a much more effective way of getting the troops moving from their slumbers. He went through their billet building with a machine gun firing through the roof shouting "there is no bloody breakfast for you lot until that roof is back on." Albert said you never saw so many men move so quickly. It was certainly a little different to running to the top of Goat Fell and back when he was on Arran.

There was also the incident about the famous cockerel weather vane on the top of the church at Somerby. The soldiers denied using it for target practice however when it came time to remove it later for maintenance purposes the evidence was plain to see. Guilty as charged was the reply.

Albert was in B Company and his Officer was W D A (Bill) Burgess who was a Royal Sussex man reflecting the class structure that was so prevalent in our forces then.

Bill had a stutter however a very brave man. He was killed at Arnhem and we always pay our respects at his grave in the Oosterbeek cemetery. A very good man who Albert highly respected.

Each week Bill would say "Sergeant, I need to address the men." Hence Albert called the men to order accordingly and Bill started to speak but after a while he started to stutter and he would turn to Sergeant Spring and say "carry on as normal Sergeant" which he duly did. This did not diminish the respect or the strict discipline that was Albert's hallmark.

Interestingly enough, one time whilst visiting Bill's grave at Oosterbeek there was a couple there and I told them the story about the weekly address and his stutter. They turned out to be his relatives and asked how I knew he had a stutter because it was not well known. So I told them the full story.

Likewise, in September 2023, Dan and I bumped into another of Bill's relatives by the name of Mark Burgess. How good is that to find someone to maintain that all important bond.

There are so many funny stories of the antics and the goings on with these so called superior Red Devils when they were based in Leicestershire.

Of a Saturday trucks would be laid on to take the men into Nottingham for some R&R which they very much looked forward to.

The problem was not getting them into Nottingham, where the ratio of ladies to men was said to be 8 to 1; the real issue was getting them back to barracks later that evening.

Father did not join those convoys but, given he was an extremely fit man, he would run into Nottingham city centre and position himself very discretely to observe who got back on the return trucks at closing time. But perhaps more importantly, he was more interested in those who did not return at the allocated time.

Father would then run back knowing exactly who was not on board.

There has been many a moan from his men of having to go on a route march in the early hours of a Sunday morning or being sent back to Nottingham to make sure their mates returned promptly or else. There was no fooling Albert and his like as they had seen it all before.

Alfred Penwill was a favourite of his as he was an older soldier as I may have said before. Now, one Sunday morning there was found a cart horse in one of the paddocks near their accommodation.

No one owned up to knowing anything about it but with Alfred being a fellow country boy from the county of Norfolk, it was a fair assumption he had missed the last truck home and had "borrowed" the cart horse to get back to Somerby.

There was nothing mentioned as to any formal disciplinary action but a quiet word in Alf's ear and the horse was returned to its rightful owner and nothing else was said!

Ironically, a number of the soldiers finished up marrying Nottingham ladies and settling in the area. One of which was the one and only Jim Westbury.

When Jim died at his home in Nottingham we all turned out for his funeral. It was obvious the Vicar did not know Jim as he addressed him as James.

After we left the crematorium we went out to look at Jim's flowers and wreaths whereupon Albert said "now let me tell you about Jim, people will tell you I favoured him. The truth is, I did, because he was the first man I turned to when it got sticky. He just loved fighting and the stickier it got the better he loved it. Every time we came upon action I used to say where is Jim? I can see Jim in action now with that Bren gun. He was the best and I did need him in the trenches with me as the saying goes." What a tribute to a special man or at least in Albert's eyes!

We enjoyed many a great time with Jim and his daughter Rona when going back to Holland. It is with great sadness I have recently found out that Rona died in August 2019. Rest in peace lovely lady.

For some reason, Jim was never keen on me because he saw me as a raging capitalist because I worked in the private sector where profit was king and, more latterly, had my own business and in Jim's eyes I was a pariah. As you may have gathered Jim was an out and out socialist working in the Post Office most of his life. He was an active shop steward in the union. He could talk for England; it is said he never lost a negotiation. His pride would not allow that as he simply wore the opposition down with words until they gave in!

Jim was big pals with Reg Shurbourne, and as I mentioned before they were in the KOYLIs together and had been pals for years.

Reg was a gentler kind who told me about them bailing out on that fateful day on the 18th September 1944. He said, "I stood at the door of the burning aircraft ready to jump backwards and I said to myself 'Reg boy this is the end of your life'. Then I jumped, the next thing I knew I hit the ground with one hell of a bang but I was alive."

Reg was a top man.

We are also still in touch with Reg's son Andy and his lovely wife Sandra. It is always good to see them.

Another of them was Fred Bramley, who Jim thought wasn't quite with it as he had to remind him on a regular basis "we are firing this way today Fred." Perhaps it was such banter that got them through it all.

For many years, Albert only told us the funny stories, then you realise there is much more to war but they didn't talk about that.

Another such character was Roy Duhamaeu from Sheffield who accused Albert, Jim, Fred and their fellow comrades in their aircraft of "drinking tea with the Dutch whilst he and his stick of Paras were fighting the bloody Germans."

I attended Roy's funeral on Albert's behalf following which I was quizzed in the normal manner "was his coffin covered with a Union Jack? Was his red beret on his coffin?" I was pleased and relieved to reply in the affirmative on both counts. They were still Albert's men up to his death in 2002. What a very special life long bond forged out of such adversity!

This was a very serious matter to Albert and, coming back to one of his fellow Para Sergeants' funeral he attended out Bedford way. Father was not impressed because there was no Union Jack or red beret.

He took the Vicar to task telling him he should be ashamed of himself for not paying the due respect this brave man deserved.

This Vicar was getting it both barrels, as Albert went on to remind him "did you know this man should have been awarded the Victoria Cross at Arnhem because he carried an Officer across that bloody bridge in the heat of the battle and then walked all the way back to Nijmegen dressed in just a trench coat. He didn't get the VC because there were no Officers to witness his actions."

There was no holding back, it simply had to be said, and that is how it was with Albert. A spade was definitely a spade. There was no compromise in such matters.

Talking of that particular Sergeant who's name escapes me. After Arnhem he decided enough was enough and he was going to go Absent Without Leave (AWOL).

His reasoning being "those Germans are good; it doesn't matter what we throw at them they keep coming back for more. I cannot see this war coming to an end soon. Hence I am going AWOL."

His mind was made up, he was not open to persuasion or for changing his mind so off he went, with the blessing of his close circle of fellow Sergeants. Indeed, it was with more than their blessing as they had a whip round to give him a few quid to send him on his way.

After a while he was caught red handed trying to break into a house in Manchester and returned to his Regiment. Hopefully, I understood this correctly but he did not lose his rank because all his fellow Sergeants gave him such glowing references. That is what real friends are for!

This goes to show that the sustained pressure of war gets to the very best of men. They are only human after all.

OPERATION MARKET GARDEN

Montgomery was keen to utilise the 25,000 or so airborne troops he had sat around in the homeland to achieve that one major breakthrough in Europe that would shorten the war.

It appears there had been many audacious plans and the best of them all was to take the three strategic bridges that gave the best chance of taking the war directly in to Germany's own back yard.

It was a risky plan because it required too many things to slot into place at the right time for it to succeed. It was principally in two parts.

Part one, Operation Market, was to take the three bridges with surprise attacks from the air using airborne troops namely Paratroopers and glider borne soldiers.

As we know there is nobody better than the airborne for such surprise incursions, however, they are only good for holding such positions for 72 hours because they are relatively lightly armed with limited resources and few in number.

Timing was everything with part two of the operation, namely Operation Garden, which required infantry troops supported by the traditional military hardware of tanks and the like to reinforce and hold those positions won by the airborne in due time.

It was crucial for these ground forces to make the necessary progress in such due time to make the plan work.

Unfortunately, the ground forces did not make the necessary progress and, it did not help, that there just happened to be a number of crack Panzer tank units resting up in around Arnhem.

Was it bad luck or was it bad planning or, as happens in business, those in charge not wishing to take any heed of information that did not fit with their plans or purposes?

Nonetheless, Operation Market Garden went ahead with the parachute and gliders drops being made over the three days of Sunday 17th, Monday 18th and Tuesday 19th September 1944.

The fact it took place over three days meant other than the first day the element of surprise was lost. Again this appears to be down to the power struggle within the Allied Supreme Command where there were huge egos conflicting with each other.

So now let us ignore the strategic stuff and tell the personal story of Albert and his cohort aboard their particular aircraft chalk mark 697.

Dan Spring's Recollections

Dan tells how Albert finished up with a bad back. When undertaking a Parachute drop he landed on top of a gate post. That must have really hurt. I can feel the pain as I write about it. Ouch, but I suspect Albert's utterances were a little stronger at the time.

All this makes me think on; I know he suffered from malaria when he was younger which presumably he caught in the African desert from the prevalent mosquitos there. We never heard him complain about it.

AIRCRAFT CHALK MARK 697

It was clear that day one on 17th September had not gone well for the Allied raiding parties, particularly at Arnhem because of there being the presence of strong German forces there; the drop zone (DZ) was too far from the bridge for that all important element of surprise and communication (or lack of) issues. Infact, it is some eleven kilometres through all sorts of terrain, which means the element of surprise simply was lost. The greatest asset of surprise that airborne troops bring was not available on this all important occasion!

Having said that, the first day was not all bad news; good progress had been made on the first two bridges at Eindhoven and Nijmegen. The problem was the third bridge, the Bridge Too Far, the ultimate prize; the bridge at Arnhem.

The 10th Battalion of the Parachute Regiment, part of the 4th Airborne Brigade, were being deployed on the second day to reinforce the surprise of the previous day.

When Albert and I first went back to Holland in 1991, the obvious question was, did you know what to expect on the second day Monday 18th September? To which he replied "yes we knew it was going to be bad because as a Stick Commander, he and his fellow leaders, had been re-briefed at midnight." I asked did it sow doubt in your mind, to which he answered "no because we could not let our first day comrades down hence our task was to simply get there and help wherever and as best we could."

Therefore, they were scheduled to take off from Spanhoe airfield early the next morning to join the battle.

When I say "they" I mean the stick of 17 Paratroopers of B Company of 10 Para with Sergeant Albert Spring as the Stick Commander.

A stick being exactly what they look like as they jump from the aircraft one after another.

Albert was a very experienced soldier and leader of men at this point having been in the army since 1940, having seen action in many theatres of war across North Africa, Egypt, the Mediterranean, the Middle East and then Italy.

He knew what it was all about.

The allocated aircraft, their means of transport to this next engagement with the enemy, was a United States Air Force (USAF) Dakota from the 315th Air Troop Carrier Command.

Their particular aircraft had been allocated the Chalk Mark number 697 which has a bit of a ring to it doesn't it. This being the number by which the aircraft and its cargo are identified. There was a degree of confusion here as inevitably there is in war missions. Perhaps a good definition is organised confusion or perhaps chaos.

This particular aircraft was crewed by the Pilot, 1st Lt James H Spurrier; the Co-Pilot 2nd Lt Edward S Fulmer (Ed to his friends), Radio Operator Corporal William T Hollis and Crew Chief with the grand name of Russell M Smith.

This was the first time this particular crew and this stick of Paras had met. It was not the first time out for the very brave aircrew. They had done a drop on the Sunday and received damage to their aircraft so I think this was the first time of being acquainted with this particular aircraft. As Ed Fulmer had said, their previous days excursion had been a reasonable ride out with not too many scares. These guys were cool dudes as the saying goes!

That day's cargo, as the Crew Chief said, consisted of the following from B Company of the 10th Battalion The Parachute Regiment.

- Sergeant Albert Spring - Stick Commander
- Sergeant Haddrell

- Sergeant Conley
- Corporal Morton
- Private Jim Westbury
- Private Reg Shurbourne
- Private Fred Bramley
- Private Norman Davies
- Private Clapperton
- Private Arnold Hayes
- Private Alfred Penwill
- Private Hare
- Lance Corporal Hodgson
- Private Wilson
- Private Clapperton
- Private Thomson
- Private Smith
- Corporal Baker

When you look at the stick list of the various aircraft there are varying numbers of Paras on each of them. I always wondered why that was. I did suggest to Albert some of the Paras may have gone AWOL on the basis they had had enough of all the false alarms and cancellations. He was having none of it. Was I doubting their professionalism?

So it will have been an early morning call for everyone as they needed to get the aircraft loaded up. The plan was to leave Spanhoe earlier in the morning however there was bad weather, fog infact, which delayed their departure.

Despite the weather, they seemed to have got away about noon. Their first destination was the rendezvous point at the Boston Stump in rural Lincolnshire. The Stump is actually St Botolph's Church, with a squat tower which makes it a significant landmark in the flat lands of the low lying fens.

Maybe as I mentioned earlier Albert said it was one of the greatest sights of his life with all these aircraft of all shapes and sizes including gliders in tow arriving and circling overhead.

Not like today in our jet engine age they were able to fly with the cargo door open.

You can imagine the spectacular sight of 1200 aircraft on a Monday lunch time circling overhead. I wonder what the local country folk must have thought of it!

Dan's Boston Stump Reflections

Verbatim they are "I've read your story so far other than spelling mistakes very good. I found the bit about Boston Stump a bit upsetting because when mum died father went to the toilet and when he came out all he could say was he was thinking back to when they were circling the Stump they were peeing in sick bags and trying to bomb the Stump. He had obviously had a few tears but that's all he said."

The time came for them to set off for their destinations. It was simple as always; they flew in formation together aiming for the middle bridge at Nijmegen, so out across the North Sea they went. Then they swapped the seascape to the flat landscape of the Netherlands, where shortly after they split up and headed off to their respective destinations; off to the right for Eindhoven, straight on down the middle for Nijmegen and diagonally left for the drop zone to the west of Arnhem.

In Albert's words they were flying on the outside of the formation going along nicely allowing him to observe the landscape and the wild life which always was close to his heart.

He said it looked so odd to see so much water where the Germans had flooded this low lying country to control its people. He saw all the cattle and animals on the strips of green that were on the higher ground above the water level.

In a strange way he found it perversely funny.

Then all hell broke loose when the anti-aircraft fire opened up. Knowing what happened subsequently I enquired if he knew they were going to be hit. To which he replied "yes because the aircraft in front of us had been literally blown out of the sky and it was our turn next."

The next thing was the front end of the plane was hit by the flak and they were in trouble. In hindsight, and despite Ed Fulmer's optimism it must have been the first burst that killed James Spurrier.

Father said there was smoke and flames everywhere and the plane was yoyoing up and down which meant they couldn't jump out.

Then the plane seemed to level up and Russell M Smith, doing his job as ever in his Tennessee drawl, instructed them in no uncertain terms to get out or words to that effect!

The Paras were all over the place as some were thrown to the floor and they were sprawled on top of each other.

One of the Paras was unlucky because a hobnail booted colleague accidentally stood on his hand and broke two or three fingers.

The plane was on fire and full of smoke so the soldiers decided to jump backwards which they duly did from a height of about 200 feet, although, I have seen reports saying it was closer to 150.

To put the height they jumped from in perspective, one time we took a guided tour of the Eusebius church in Arnhem itself.

When we were about half way up the inside of the spire Jim Westbury quipped to Albert "do you realise we are further off the ground than when we jumped in 1944."

Whichever way, it was much lower than planned or safe so to do.

Nonetheless they did it relatively successfully with much more calmness and assurance than anyone could have been expected.

Before we get into the detail the best version of events I have seen is in a book kindly sent to me by Laura Briggs of the USAF 315th Troop Carrier Command who's grandad, Captain Paul Melucas, was also a pilot on this particular mission. It wasn't him, but one of the other pilots who was flying in the same formation saw aircraft 697 peel away on fire and in serious trouble.

The next thing the pilot and crew saw was the plane hit the ground and burst into flames. He subsequently reported there could not have been any survivors. However, to everyone's surprise there were.

Now, that is an interesting point because it is said that our mum received a telegram saying her husband was missing in action when she was eight months pregnant with their second child. How is that for stress and pressure on a mega scale?

Of the seventeen Paras, sixteen made it to the ground safely and reasonably well. There were one or two with damaged ankles, broken legs and the like.

To use Jim Westbury parlance, he reckoned Albert broke his leg on impact, but as Jim said, Sergeants don't admit to broken legs; and went on to add at least he had the thinnest sandwiches ever from his squashed ration tin strapped to his leg!

The seventeenth Paratrooper was Alfred Penwill who's chute did not open properly. There are reports it may have caught the nearby overhead power lines.

Sadly, Alf had fallen the best part of two hundred feet and not even superman could have survived that.

As I said before Albert was close to Alf (he really liked him given he was the same age and he too was a married man). I am sure I recall him saying he jumped alongside Alf and witnessed him hit the ground.

Father said all the records show you cannot fall from such a height and not be killed instantly.

However, as his Sergeant, Albert went straight to him and whilst he was in a very bad way with multiple injuries he was still alive.

He said "Albert, what have I done?" Albert gave him a morphine injection from his emergency first aid kit and Alf died ten minutes later.

After the Paras had jumped Ed Fulmer was still at the controls, and despite his injuries, was trying to crash land the plane so he could save his buddy James Spurrier by getting him out of the burning wreck.

Ed said that was his top priority and the Paras came second in his thoughts at the time which is understandable given the horror of trying to save his friend.

He did manage to clip the pylon carrying the overhead power lines running parallel to the adjacent road towards Arnhem which slowed the plane down. Now whether that was luck or great judgement who will ever know but it did give Ed the best chance of saving Spurrier.

Upon reflection, it also, unwittingly, gave Ed the best chance of survival too but he wasn't thinking about that at the time.

The wreck was on fire and, after realising Spurrier was dead, it was all about getting himself out of the wreck. Whilst there are several versions of what may have happened, Ed did get out and managed to stagger towards some local Dutch people nearby who dowsed him down and took him away.

His action was of the highest order imaginable. His bravery and cool thinking under the greatest possible pressure was insane. It was truly outstanding.

Given Crew Chief Smith had literally thrown the Paras out and the plane was descending, he and Hollis were instructed to bail out by Co Pilot Fulmer.

Fortunate for the Crew Chief, he did hit the ground with one hell of a thud but he was still alive albeit with a broken ankle.

Hollis was not so lucky as his chute had barely opened when he hit the ground and he died almost immediately because of the huge impact.

More about the American aircrew later but suffice to say they put the Paras before themselves and at the same time demonstrated courage and bravery above the call of any man. The respect from the likes of myself, my brother Dan and indeed Albert and all the Red Devils that day, is of the highest order.

We have reached the point where the aircraft or at least what was left of it, along with the aircrew and Para cargo, was on the ground in one way or another behind enemy lines.

BEHIND ENEMY LINES

So there they were, regrouped in an unknown field armed to their back teeth, ready to kill anybody, sixteen British Paratroopers on Dutch soil behind enemy lines. To be honest they weren't quite sure where they were but attack was the best form of defence and indeed survival.

At this point, I always say that Hans Vervoorn, a 21 year old medical student, saved the lives of Albert and his comrades. If you think about it, Hans saved himself and his fellow Dutch Resistance members as well, who came towards the highly suspicious soldiers in that field that particular afternoon.

The Paras had their guns cocked and ready for action when this young man started whistling a tune that sounded like God Save the King.

Albert being very alert heard this familiar sound and said, "hang on, they might be on our side, so do not shoot."

His hunch served him well as it turned out they were from the local branch of the Dutch Resistance including amongst others; Hans, Johannes van Zanten, Fre de Jong and Harry Tomesen.

After breaking the ice the Resistance group explained their purpose and plan, they were escorted away under the cover of dusk to a local farmhouse called the Hazenhof on the outskirts of the village of Kesteren, where it was agreed the farmer would forego their home in aid of the greater cause.

Ironically, the Hazenhof was located across the road from the local German headquarters who were a little suspicious of the comings and goings and decided to investigate a little further. Upon approaching the house, the so called farmer came out to approach them in a distressed state, he was emotional because as he explained his daughter had died the night before from diphtheria and here was the doctor's certificate to confirm the same.

The Germans had a total aversion to any such fatal diseases. Hence, they made a hasty retreat as the last thing they wanted was to catch it.

Unbeknown to them, only a few yards away were 16 enemy Paratroopers plus one injured USAF crew chief. The so called farmer was none other than a man I only knew as the Kangaroo, a member of Johannes van Zanten's resistance group.

Albert struck a chord with the Kangaroo because he, like Albert, was a man of the countryside which is a polite way of saying he was a poacher like himself. I am reliably informed his proper name is Hanje van der Voort, the 'Kangaroo' fruit merchant residing in the town of Kesteren. His nickname came from his football skills. And I quote, he could make fast 'looks' to outsmart his opponents.

Upon meeting with him again in 1991 that bond was obvious from these two country folk.

In a nutshell, the raiders were living behind enemy lines and being protected by the Resistance.

Albert's instructions were clear, if you cannot get to the drop zone at Ginkel Heath or the bridge at Arnhem, then you must carry out local reconnaissance and feed the information back through the Dutch Resistance.

The men of 697 were some thirty kilometres short of the drop zone and it would be extremely dangerous to get there on foot, for not only the Paras but also the Dutch people, because the Germans had a dreadful habit of taking their revenge against the civilian population.

Therefore, Albert, being the diligent non-commissioned Officer he was, did just that. His routine consisted of changing from his army uniform into Dutch civilian clothes acting as a deaf and dumb Dutchman.

This of course was extremely dangerous because if he had gotten caught he would have been exterminated on the spot. But this was Albert doing his duty and not thinking about the cost to himself.

A priority to him was doing the right thing by Alfred Penwill, as a result of which Albert took a serious calculated risk in attending his funeral in Opheusden, dressed in civilian clothes, which was conducted by the locals under the supervision of the German soldiers who were in attendance.

Upon getting back to England, Albert wrote to both Alfred's parents and his wife, who I understand was expecting their first child. In those letters he explained he had attended the funeral hence knew exactly where Alfred was buried.

This is Albert, the tough battle hardened soldier, showing his compassionate and caring side for his men who were much more than mere soldiers to him.

This mention of compassion and caring for his men reminds me of a conversation between Roy Gregory, a fellow Paratrooper with Albert, and my brother Dan on the occasion of Albert's surprise eightieth birthday in 1996. It went like this;

Roy said "Dan, your father was the best Sergeant we had because he cared for and looked after us." What a compliment to pay anyone particularly at a time of a dispassionate world.

It appears not all the other Sergeants showed these all important traits as there were stories of the ordinary soldiers being exposed to danger rather needlessly.

That is how Albert remained all his life; once a friend always a friend, and they came first. They were always his men.

However there were exceptions, particularly if you got the wrong side of him.

As a classic example there were two fellow Sergeants in their stick. Albert got word via Jim Westbury these two were of the view that the party should surrender given the imminent danger and impossible circumstances.

He took them aside where they confirmed their preference. Albert reminded them, in no uncertain terms, of their collective orders. You do not surrender under any circumstances; you fight to the bitter end. If you still wish to surrender then I interpret that as disobeying orders and I will shoot you myself.

They decided surrendering was not such a good idea after all! And more importantly, Albert never spoke of these two well respected soldiers again. I have to admit I have exactly this same trait. The question being is this a strength or a weakness?

THE HAZENHOF

Jim Westbury was always the story teller and he told one or two about their stay at Hazenhof.

One of which featured the back door there. Given the location adjacent to the Germans and the simple fact that they were hidden behind enemy lines, security and obeying instructions was super important.

For anybody who knows the farmhouse will realise it has a prominent front door facing the road. Hence for obvious reasons the sensible means of access was the back door, used by the farmer for his animals, which is much more discrete.

Given Jim was one of Albert's trusties he was given clear instructions. "Jim, you guard that door with your life. If anybody comes anywhere near it you let them have it, no questions asked."

Subsequently, in the early hours of the morning, the door flew open and there stood Albert with a broad grin on his face and said "Jim, I knew I could rely on you to disobey my orders."

The Hazenhof was a working farm back in those days and indeed to the rear of the house was where the cows and horses were housed. If you go back to the house the names of the animals were preserved on the timber beams for each of the stalls.

Hans Vervoorn was very impressed with the British soldiers and was determined to treat them to a traditional bacon and eggs breakfast. As you can imagine, laying on a traditional English breakfast for sixteen fighting men was no small fry up.

Equally, the aroma from the wonderful feast was an issue but Hans, a 21 year old young man, knew no bounds regardless of the dangers of such a delight.

The breakfast was duly served without amiss much to the satisfaction of everyone. Hans saw it as mission accomplished and the guests were delighted with their hearty breakfast!

Since Albert's return to Holland in 1991, we have always enjoyed our visits there. It always felt like home. This was very much down to the wonderful hospitality of Jan and Sophie van Velzen who lived there on our first visit through to more recently.

They were the most wonderful hosts, whether it be a more formal visit to unveil the plaque at the front door or just dropping in for a social chat. Jan and Sophie's hospitality and warmth was always so special. They looked after Albert, Jim Westbury, Ed Fulmer and their entourage so well.

Not only was the farmhouse their beautiful home, but more importantly for us, they understood its history and significance in the war and to us families of those very brave men from those few days in September 1944. They even had a decorative parachute hanging there!

Jan always made sure Dan got his dark beer albeit it is no longer available.

We enjoyed many a visit sat in the rear yard enjoying the beautiful cakes and drinks and swapping stories with the likes of Jan and Sophie, Mike and Anne Hayes, Andy and Sandy Shurbourne along with our children. It literally felt like home from home.

Sadly Jan and Anne Hayes are no longer with us but they will never be forgotten.

We last saw Jan with Sophie at their new home in Nijmegen in September 2022. Sadly, Jan died shortly after then. What a truly remarkable man.

For the record, the Paras called the Hazenhof their home for a total of three nights, Monday 18th, Tuesday 19th and Wednesday 20th September 1944 then leaving to make their escape on the night of the 21st. Having said that there was always a difference between the recollections of Albert and Hans as to the exact length of their stay but I don't think anybody was counting.

Now there are new owners so our ability to visit our Dutch 'home' is in question. Regardless, the Hazenhof will always have a very special place in our hearts.

We cannot thank the Dutch people including Jan and Sophie enough.

THE REMARKABLE BRAVERY OF THE AMERICAN AIRCREW

Edward Simons Fulmer

As part of his duties it was important to Albert to know how Ed Fulmer was, given he was at the front end of the plane that took the worst of the anti-aircraft fire and the impact. Albert realised the bravery and the remarkable actions of this very special young man had provided the opportunity for the soldiers to bail out to relative safety.

If they had crash landed with the aircraft it would most certainly resulted in them all being killed.

Ed had been spirited away by the local Resistance members to the cellar of a Doctor van Empel nearby because he needed treatment for his various wounds, let alone the trauma of what this remarkable young man had been through.

Then, like now, nothing was as simple in those dreadful days of war and occupation by the hated enemy. It was all about the community pulling together to provide the best form of protective shield possible. This included the children alike, one of whom went by the name of Nellie Silstra, who was about seven or eight years old at the time.

As a footnote, we met Nellie in the 1990s at her home. What a fabulous lady who could recall those dim and distant days and this particular incident.

Nellie's instructions were very straightforward; play as normal and if you see German soldiers or strange people then sing this particular song to provide warning to those in the doctor's surgery and elsewhere. Forewarned is forearmed.

Nellie did her job beautifully. Presumably, she sang her song dutifully when two strangers in civilian clothes appeared in the street. I understand there was a degree of consternation on this particular occasion when the strangers approached the doctors house as they were not wearing uniforms!

They need not have worried, because it was only Albert in civilian clothes, with a member of the Resistance. One was a Dutchman and the other a pretend Dutchman!

Albert was here to check up on his pilot friend. After the initial exchanges he asked, "how is he doctor?" to which came the reply "he has two injured legs, two injured arms, bullet wounds through his backside (bottom), his front teeth have been shot out and he has burns to 65% to his body area. Other than that he is fine."

As I write this, I feel the tingle of emotion within in me nearly eighty years later. What must it have been like in the raw emotion on that day! Albert then was not an emotional man but I understand he was on this occasion.

Ed, whilst not in his best of health physically and emotionally, was surprised and very pleased to see the leader of the Paras.

Infact it is quoted that the British Sergeant's visit had done Ed more good than any doctors medicine or treatment!

Forgive the pun, but what a shot in the arm for this hero all the way from Syracuse in New York State in the United States of America.

The strength of the bond between Ed and Albert was forged so strongly between them at that particular moment and endured until they died but they hardly knew each other.

Isn't that amazing?

What was not apparent at that time was the full extent of Ed's injuries over and above those previously mentioned.

These only became apparent later. The physical impact of the aircraft hitting the ground had caused him to develop arthritis subsequently, which meant in later life, he spent long periods in a wheelchair. The hidden consequences of such bravery!

He also told me that he struggled with concentration and being able to settle after the war. This is not an unusual phenomenon in such circumstances.

Albert knew about Ed's arthritis issues because when they wrote to each other Ed's letters took days and indeed weeks to compose because of the arthritis in his hands limiting the amount of writing he could do at any one time.

His post-crash repatriation experiences were interesting. He was first returned to England and then to the United States for further hospitalisation and recuperation. He said his parents were trying to find him, thinking he was still overseas, when he was infact, back in the States, as a result of which they were not reacquainted for the best part of a year.

Strange things happen in war and stranger things happen as a consequence. Edward Simons Fulmer being a good case in point!

Oddly enough, Ed's repatriation from behind enemy lines was straight forward. An ambulance simply called at the property where he was being looked after, loaded him in then drove him to Allied territory, which goes to show luck and timing can be on your side, even in the depths of such adversity.

Of all the survivors of this horrific incident, the one you would have put your money on to leave us first was Ed Fulmer, given his extensive injuries. But no, he was made of sterner stuff than that because he outlived them all to reach the ripe old age of ninety nine.

When he died 31st December 2017 he was buried with full military honours; no more than this super hero richly deserved.

When we met him, it struck me he was so un-American. I hope I do not upset my American friends. He was extremely modest, played down his heroism to the point we had to cajole him into wearing his richly deserved medals. More of that later.

James Spurrier, Russell M Smith & William Hollis

We cannot leave this point without mentioning the other aircrew.

Firstly, the pilot James Spurrier who was killed by anti-aircraft fire. He was clearly a very experienced pilot and a big buddy of Ed's.

I find it strange the dead seem to get forgotten or pushed into the background in war. The dead are the dead, but I don't see it like that because they did literally give their lives for our freedom.

So, when the occasion arose to be in the south of the Netherlands in 2007 I took the opportunity to visit James' grave in the American cemetery in Margraten to pay my respects. To my complete surprise I found him buried next to his brother, also killed over Europe, in the same month of September 1944. At least these brothers were at peace together but what about their dear parents?

Radio Operator William Hollis, as we know, was killed on the drop and again I visited his grave to show my respects. His gravestone stands alone. It made me wonder what he looked like and what he was all about, as he was a young man at the end of the day. Thank you so much young man for giving your life so others, such as my father, had a better chance of living.

Russell M Smith, although he sustained a broken ankle, was repatriated to England where he and Ed Fulmer met up. Given Albert's impression of him I imagine him have been as big and as brave as John Wayne. He certainly wasn't having any nonsense from these cocky Red Devils; get out meant get out and no messing!

Maybe, I haven't done justice to these remarkably brave airmen, however, Albert was questioned about the incident of 697 when he got back to the UK in 1944.

He told me he was commanded to meet a group of Officers who wanted to know exactly what had happened in great detail.

Albert did not know the purpose of the interrogation, and admitted he thought he was in trouble because, perhaps he could, and should have done more to join the battle?

After the interrogation, he was relieved to learn the interrogators were more interested in the bravery of the American aircrew.

Father would have been meticulous in his evidence because that was so typical of him.

We did not know until much later that all four of the American aircrew were awarded the United States Congressional Medal of Honour as a result of our father's recommendation.

How remarkable is that?

As a result and furthermore, Ed Fulmer was made a Knight in the Military Order of William from the Netherlands. This is the oldest and highest honour of the Kingdom of the Netherlands. We were rubbing shoulders with a Knight no less!

This meant that Ed, and his lovely wife Lucille, were guests of the King or Queen whenever they visited the Netherlands.

Can you imagine our pride in knowing the formal recognition of these extremely brave people came from our dad!

And the British gave them nothing! But why? Jim Westbury, in his eloquent manner explained it away in no uncertain terms.

He said these men richly deserved bravery awards, however, this was not possible because such awards in the eyes of the British can only be given if witnessed by an Officer and a gentleman. As Jim put it, our Sergeant failed on both counts!

It was no wonder that Albert was made an honorary member of the 315th Troop Carrier Command.

DOING RECONNAISSANCE

As before, Albert's priority was carrying out reconnaissance and feeding it back through the Dutch Resistance. This involved getting out there in his civilian disguise to see what was going on. He couldn't do it alone so the likes of Hans Vervoorn, Harry Tomeson and Fre de Jong would join him.

These memories of their adventures come to mind.

One night when they were patrolling together in a motor vehicle they came across a Resistance checkpoint. The vehicle came to a halt and one of the Dutch men got out and spoke to their colleagues guarding the checkpoint. Upon his return to the vehicle he reported they would not let them through.

Upon hearing this Albert jumped out of the back of the car and, after a short exchange, they were waved through.

Upon his return to the car Albert explained he had simply shown them his gun and they kindly agreed to let them through. What was the problem?

Another occasion, out in the beautiful Dutch countryside in broad daylight on their bikes, with Albert in his deaf and dumb Dutchman guise, they came across some German soldiers. A healthy discussion soon started between the Dutch and the Germans. Albert, being the ever professional soldier, happened to have a hand grenade in his pocket, just in case!

Voices were raised and Albert was a little concerned so he slowly withdrew the safety pin from the grenade. A seasoned soldier of his standing can do these sort of things without anyone noticing. Perhaps, like someone peeling an orange.

Thankfully, things calmed down and everybody went their very own ways.

As Albert cycled down the road he explained his concern and mentioned the pin less grenade in his pocket.

To which Hans responded, "throw it in that water below the dike and pedal like hell!"

JOHANNES VAN ZANTEN & HIS BOYS

Before we get into the detail, it is important to explain the members of the Dutch Resistance were not professionally trained soldiers, unlike all the aircrew and the Paras. It is important to make this very important distinction from the outset.

These remarkable people were doing it for their love of their country and their hatred of the enemy.

Johannes van Zanten

The leader of this particular group or cell of the Dutch Resistance was Johannes van Zanten.

He was a married man in his early thirties, with five children under the age of ten, who lived in Kesteren in the Neder Betuwe which lay below the flight path of the air train to Arnhem.

He was dedicated to the cause of freedom for his beloved Netherlands, some would say perhaps too much so given his responsibilities as a husband and a parent.

Albert thought very highly of him because he was a man he trusted who got things done in extremely difficult circumstances.

His bravery was second to none. A story that comes to mind that demonstrates this goes like this;

The Germans had been suspicious of Johannes' loyalty. In order to show this wasn't the case, he invited one of the locally based German Officers to join him and his family for a meal and drinks one evening. The soldier enjoyed the hospitality so much that he actually fell asleep in front of a nice hot fire.

He had placed his revolver on the table on arrival and when he fell asleep Van Zanten could easily have shot him with his own gun. But he didn't and when the Officer awoke Van Zanten said "how can

I be against you because I could easily have shot you whilst you were asleep?"

They were not convinced as they were hugely suspicious of his intentions and his deeds.

The family home was located adjacent to the local cemetery where, ironically, the great man is buried. Within this consecrated area there are a number of above ground burial tombs within which, it is said, he stored the guns used by the Resistance fighters.

He was a well-respected local man as the leader of the Resistance. Albert spent quite a bit of time with him hence the total respect he had for Johannes because he was the architect of the protection of many of the Allied forces in Operation Market Garden.

The likes of Hans, Harry, Fre and the Kangaroo were his boys. Their loyalty was steadfast in very dangerous circumstances.

There is so much more to him, his achievements and in the end, his very sad demise.

Our dear friend Conny van der Heyden has written a brilliant book dedicated to the story of this man.

I do not profess to know the full story but as I understand it he was arrested when he attended a meeting in Utrecht in late 1944 and taken away for interrogation by the Germans. This led to him being executed in Apeldoorn on 2nd December 1944.

This was an extremely sad day for the whole family, the community of Neder Betuwe and the Dutch resistance.

There are photos of his funeral when he was eventually buried in the very same cemetery in Kesteren. If you get the chance, then please do take the opportunity to visit his grave to remember a true hero.

We, as a family, are very thankful for all Johannes did for Albert and his men because without his bravery and leadership Dan and I might not be here.

That is why Albert always made it his business to place flowers on his grave and have a quiet word. We still continue that duty again out of thanks and respect for our super hero. The bond is so strong not just with Johannes, but also with his family and children. It is the ultimate tie that binds.

No wonder he was awarded the highest Netherlands civilian bravery award; the Bronze Lion.

Hans Vervoorn

Hans Vervoorn became Professor of Tropical Medicine given he was trained as a doctor after the war.

He was also a young man who had very firm views about his country, the Netherlands and, in particular their arch enemy, the Germans. He, like so many other young Dutch people, were given the opportunity to sign their allegiance to the so called mother nation of Germany. Hans chose not to do that and as a result was, effectively, on the run and homeless.

That is where his allegiance to his home country came from and why he became a member of the Dutch Resistance working with Johannes van Zanten in the Neder Betuwe region.

I have already told the story of how this twenty one year old man, for all intentions, saved the lives of those survivors from Chalk Mark 697 and, no doubt, many other liberators who finished up behind enemy lines in a rather similar perilous position.

Hans had never forgotten those airborne soldiers from those fateful days and, in particular, Albert. When it came time for the so called escape from the Hazenhof back to Allied territory he told me those soldiers were so professional, well organised without any signs of fear or worry. He called them proper men and he said the escape was like a stroll in the park to them.

Hans told of his work with the likes of Harry and Fre as well as Johannes in not only protecting those service men but also feeding and providing accommodation for them.

Those Dutch boys went to great lengths to provide rations. And, may I say, at great personal risk too. They were extremely brave.

The thought of the consequences of them getting apprehended by their occupiers did not bear thinking about. It could have meant instant death.

Hans was a very proud Dutchman. He was rather put out that father and I brought flowers from England to put on the graves of the likes of Penwill and Van Zanten. He made his point very strongly by saying "do you not know the Dutch grow the best flowers in the world?" Therefore all future flowers and wreaths were sourced in Holland under the careful supervision of one extremely proud Dutchman!

There were similar debates and positions regarding whether BP (British Petroleum) petrol for my car was better than Dutch Shell when I was filling up!

After the war and upon qualifying as a Doctor Hans worked in the likes of Indonesia. He told stories of his time as a doctor in Africa when the infamous Idi Amin was in power in Uganda.

He told the story of this dictator's troops hunting down his critics / enemies. On one occasion he and his wife Wil hid one such person behind their stove in their home whilst he was being hunted. Tremendous bravery and, like Albert, if he had been caught it would have been at great personal risk.

Let me introduce his wife Wil, who was such a wonderful lady by the way she looked after Albert and everyone, when we stayed with them in their home in Amersfoort.

Wil and Hans had travelled widely as part of his career.

We first met them in May 1991 when Albert returned for the very first time.

There was no kinder lady than Wil, and, it was with extreme sadness, when we learned of her unexpected passing many years ago.

There will be much more about Hans as we progress through time. If it had not been for him hunting down the reluctant Albert we may never have known his and their story and their parts together all those years earlier. Hence, we owe Hans and Wil so much for making it happen at the time and subsequently.

It is also important to recognise the legacy that Hans and Wil passed on with the creation of our long term friendship and bond with their children namely Lieke, Majorke and Hans Junior, and their families.

Hans was awarded the much deserved Bronze Lion bravery award for his outstanding service after the war.

On a lighter note, when we were planning our first visit in 1991 father and I discussed gifts and, not knowing them from Adam, we settled on a nice bottle of Scotch whisky for Hans. When we presented it to him he said I don't drink whisky as I am beer drinker. So the next time over we presented him with an engraved glass beer tankard. He was much happier with that!

As a foot note I was so proud and honoured to be invited to speak at this great man's funeral on the subject of "Our Fathers."

Fre De Jong

I always saw Fre as a quiet man, however, his son Arjen de Jong assures me he wasn't. He loved his motorbikes so it seems and could be found stood on the seat whilst driving through the Dutch countryside. Perhaps not quite as shy or quiet as I thought!

He was also a very caring man inasmuch when van Zanten lost his life Fre would help Mrs van Zanten to look after the children.

There was a lot more to him than met the eye. My lasting memory was accompanying him to the front door of the cottage in Boven-Leeuwen near where the Paras were taken after crossing the River Waal. This lady came to the door and said "oh Fre, it is so good to see you again after all this time. We still have the ornament you gave us for letting you stay with us when you brought those Paras over the river all those years ago."

A rather special man, who we are eternally grateful to for everything he did for Albert and everyone involved.

Harry Tomeson

My first memory of Harry was him arriving at one of the Burgemeester's receptions in 1991, having been delayed in traffic, travelling up from his home in Bergen Op Zoom.

As he entered the room Albert stepped towards him, shook his hand and said "Harry, I am so pleased to see you again after all this time." They had last met in 1944. Isn't that some special bond of the strongest possible kind.

As I recall, Harry was the head of our equivalent of a technical college in the Netherlands.

He had struggled with his sleep because of what happened during the war. This went on for over forty years when it was suggested to him that writing down such memories may be a good way to overcome those demons. This he duly did, and I know Hans Vervoorn certainly had a copy of it because, with it being in Dutch, he translated that part of it to English in manuscript where Albert gets a mention from all those years previously.

This is where my previous story about them getting through the Resistance checkpoint came from. I still have a copy, and I must look it up, if I can read Han's best doctor's hand writing!

Albert held Harry in very high regard, I can remember him insisting on one of our visits that we travel down to Harry's home town of Bergen Op Zoom to lay a wreath out of respect to this special man who had died more recently.

Other Dutch Heroes

Hopefully, I have given a mention to most of those involved, however, if I have failed to mention a few that I should have done from those times then, my humble apologies.

I can recall us attending a ceremony to remember some of those exceptionally brave people who rowed the Paras across the River Waal in the pitch black of the middle of the night of 22nd / 23rd September 1944. What a remarkable feat and what bravery?

Albert always insisted there was another member of the Resistance there on the 18th September but Hans said there wasn't. This is the problem with the workings of the memories and imaginations over the passage of time.

Nonetheless, huge thanks go to all those people who took part and showed such courage and bravery. We owe you so much.

THE ESCAPE

There was growing concern the Germans may have been getting more and more suspicious of the goings on at the Hazenhof.

It was not simply a case of what would happen to the locals if it was found they had been assisting the Allies. The Germans were well renowned for their reprisals against any act of resistance or even simply not cooperating.

It is important to remember the region of Neder Betuwe and Kesteren and Opheusden in particular were very quiet areas where the predominant activity was agriculture and growing trees.

Therefore the last thing they wanted was more trouble than they already had particularly if it meant the Germans taking innocent people from their homes or even worse.

Therefore van Zanten and his men put plans in place to move the military personnel to safer ground as a priority.

The plan consisted of the cohort travelling by foot for the best part of eight kilometres to the bank of the big wide River Waal where they would be transported by boat at night to the Allied territory on the other bank in the region of Boven-Leeuwen where they would be taken to a safe factory.

The route followed the local railway line for quite a distance which was good because the embankment formed a natural protective barrier for the group of twenty or so men who were carrying their equipment such as guns which they had not fired in anger.

There is another one of Jim's stories about the escape, or at least the journey over the terra firmer. As mentioned previously, Jim was an excellent performer with his beloved Bren gun and he loved nothing better than going into action against the old adversary. On this occasion, alas, it was not to be, nonetheless, Jim always carried his beloved weapon ready for action.

It is important to remember the enemy were on their case now and, as I understand, they were using searchlights to find them.

On this particular occasion Jim was itching for a bit of action and whispered to his Sergeant Albert "let me have a go at them" to which Albert replied "Jim, now is not the time or place."

So all those many years, indeed decades later, Jim moaned "I carried that bloody gun all the way from England to Holland and back and never fired a bloody shot." He was not a happy bunny and he certainly had not forgotten!

So they made their way to the banks of the Waal via a brick factory where the escapees and the Resistance men rendezvoused with the boatmen.

It is said they crossed in two or three rowing boats, just like the more recent enactment organised so well by Gerard Nieuwenhuis and his colleagues.

This was in the silence and depth of darkness of the early hours of the morning.

It is important to remember the River Waal must be at least two hundred yards wide at this point. This is one of the major waterways of Europe let alone Holland. Anything could happen.

We have stood there on a number of occasions in wonder of the achievement particularly in the middle of the night.

Another of Jim Westbury's pearls of wisdom applies at this particular time; Jim said he now knew how Washington felt when he crossed the River Delaware centuries earlier!

Only Jim could have been thinking of anything other than getting across this great expanse of water to safety. I am pretty sure Albert would not have given a monkeys about what Washington was up to or even thinking about!

Thenkfully, they made it to the other side without incident where they were to be met by another group of the Resistance.

Given the lack of trust, indeed treachery within the Resistance, who could you trust? That was exactly the question I put to Albert to which he replied, "we didn't trust any of them, I knew what the passwords were on arrival on the other side, and if they were not produced as planned or anything suspicious happened then we were going to let them all have it as we didn't trust any of them at this point."

Again this is the reality of war and, perhaps, the mentality of the trained seasoned professional soldier versus the volunteer Resistance worker.

Thankfully the right words were said and they came ashore without incident.

In my cabinet at home I have a heavy figure of a Stormtroopen who were the local Dutch guards of the banks of the River Waal. It was presented to Albert on the fiftieth anniversary of the end of the war or was it the fiftieth anniversary of the battle of Arnhem. Albert, and all his comrades were Waal Crossers which is no mean feat. Hence, I am very proud of their achievement.

Is there anything such as the perfect plan?

The soldiers next destination was a factory not far from the river bank however a German Officer had defected in the previous few hours and had turned himself in at the very same factory. This whole episode was viewed with great suspicion hence the final rendezvous point was changed at the last minute to a farm house further down the track.

Albert, in his capacity as the leader, was involved in various discussions with Allied soldiers and members of the Resistance. However, this was the point where they felt relatively safe and it was time to say thank you and goodbye. Would you believe they were not to meet again until some forty six years later.

I told you the story about Fre de Jong and the house nearby. There is also a funny story, or funny of sorts, involving Hans Vervoorn. Whilst Hans was a clever and resolute man it appears swimming was not a particular strength. However, his instructions were clear; he was to swim back across the mighty River Waal, rest up and let his clothes dry and pretend he was a farmers boy looking after a herd of cows that did not exist.

Herdsman Vervoorn went about his new found profession after he had rested up and dried out whereupon he came across some German soldiers who, when he told them his forlorn story, helped him try to find his fictious herd. Alas, they could not find them so off he trundled.

To conclude the escape after the various discussions the men were loaded on Allied trucks and transported to Nijmegen prior to being flown back to England. This was except one of the Paras; the one who had his fingers broken when they were trampled in the burning aircraft. Thomson was his name. I understand when he got to Nijmegen, Albert told him to jump on a truck which was going to the local hospital to get his damaged fingers seen to. Paradoxically and sadly, the truck was bombed and all those on board were killed. Another massive irony of war.

RETURNING TO SOMERBY

The people of Somerby and Burrough on the Hill and the surrounding area had been home to the men of the 10th. In those few months this community had taken them to their hearts. These men were fighting for our freedom. The stakes could not be higher.

These men had that something special about them as they were proud Paras, they had been referred to as the Red Devils by their fiercest of enemies.

They also had that cockiness of being seen as elite and indeed, dare I say, special. This brought out their unique character and personality which endeared them to the hearts of the local folk.

Hence, these locals were planning the biggest and the best homecoming party for their heroes.

After all, the numbers quoted vary but as I understand it 580 men had left this beautiful countryside to go and do their business but only 43 came back. That does not mean they all perished. 110 men lost their lives with the rest being taken prisoners of war.

Thankfully 15 of the 43 were from chalk mark 697 including Albert. This is another irony of fighting, with their aircraft having been in danger of crashing and everybody lost. Because of the actions of so many special people they survived where many others perished.

There is a strong analogy here with Albert's experience on the Litani River raid some three years earlier. There he lost the best part of two hundred of his comrades, indeed, friends, and on this occasion it was over one hundred of them gone forever and a great deal of uncertainty about the other four hundred or so of his comrades.

This must have been the ultimate test of character and mind.

As was typical of Albert's pragmatic way he said at least there was plenty to eat!

Clearly, this was the end of the very proud The 10th Battalion The Parachute Regiment. Leaving a very proud legacy of a fine fighting force. These were no ordinary men. As I recall in those immortal words, Every Man An Emperor!

Through these experiences those remaining men were bonded together forever.

This statement sums up the men of the 10th.

> "Born in the desert,
> Flowered in Italy,
> Withered at Arnhem,
> Yet did not die"

Indeed, those survivors who made it back did not die, they went on to other Regiments because they were professional soldiers and their and our freedom was not yet won. The bright idea of shortening the war came at one hell of a price.

Closer to home on the family front, Albert and Olive welcomed their second son Arthur Edward Spring on 19th October 1944 some 31 days after dad had been declared missing in action.

The full swing of emotions from despair to joy in effectively one month; how does the human mind deal with that?

Me, my brothers and our Dad, owe our mum Edith Olive so much. No wonder our mum is one of my super heroes.

It was not an easy life being the only female in a world with five men.

Thank you mum, I wish I had understood all this at the time. That is the benefit of time, hindsight and realisation. We owe you so much.

No wonder you made so much fuss of my daughter Emma, who, her Grandma Spring is one of her very few super heroes, even to this day.

I digress, there was joy in the Spring household on the day Arthur was born.

WHAT NEXT FOR ALBERT

The men of the 10th were assigned to their new roles in the fight for survival.

It is also important to remember it wasn't just the 10th that took a battering at Arnhem.

Hence, Albert's next destination was to be with the 2nd Battalion The Parachute Regiment. The very same Battalion that took the bridge at Arnhem under the leadership of none other than John Frost.

I do not know too much about Albert's time with them. However, there were one or two anecdotes from him. Given all the losses and missions that had not gone well it struck me the obvious question was, had he ever been frightened?

Even if he was frightened it would take one hell of a lot to drag such an admission out of this very proud, battle hardened and insular man. He was his own rock who kept his own council. His life experiences had forged him that way.

Hence, I was surprised at his response to my question. Albert said he was frightened once in February 1945 when they were based in barracks on Salisbury Plain in Wiltshire.

He said it was the middle of winter, it was freezing cold, there was snow on the ground and he had been briefed about undertaking a parachute drop in the Ardennes, a forested area in Belgium.

So what caused his fright? Surprisingly, it was simply the fact that his men were relatively new recruits that he did not know who did not have the experience of his tried and trusted men of B Company of the 10th.

It wasn't the task. It was the resource he was being given to deliver it with. Ironically the operation did not happen, like so many others!

This is a perfect example of Albert being a man's man. He could forgive their faubles because he knew he could trust them implicitly.

The analogy is with starting a new demanding job after many years of working with a tried and trusted team albeit the stakes then were literally a matter of life and death.

Another story he mentioned related to how he saw his war experience.

It relates to the return of the soldiers from the Far East therefore it must have been later in 1945 when the war in Europe was over.

He was asked, amongst others, to undertake a demonstration Parachute drop in Scotland to the returning soldiers from the Far East

Whilst we think Paratroopers have been a fighting force forever, let us remind ourselves they were, after all, an invention of the Second World War. Hence, as part of the welcoming home party it was deemed a great idea to show these men our new proud invention of Paratroopers.

Albert, and his comrades, duly did their duty to show off those airborne soldiers jumping out of aeroplanes as a means of going to war.

The demonstration drops were followed by a few drinks in the mess to socialise with the returning heroes. Albert said they spoke to them but there was no response. He said you could speak to them as they were physically there but their minds had gone.

Albert said he suddenly realised he had had a good war; despite the fact he had seen more than his fair share of death and destruction including losing many of his close and dear friends.

Regardless of that the reality was that Albert still had his mind whereas those men had lost theirs because of what they had seen and endured in the Far East. Again an example of the reality of consequences of war.

For me, the culmination of his time with 2 Para is a photo I have which was taken on 17th September 1945. It is of the famous and very proud Second Battalion The Parachute Regiment marching through London commemorating the first anniversary of the day they took the bridge at Arnhem.

Out front is the famous John Frost with Albert, my dad, on the front row. I cannot tell you how proud I am of him.

A remarkable achievement for a humble country boy from Winwick.

It goes to reinforce the statement 'he must have been good because they did not suffer fools gladly.' John Frost certainly did not suffer fools gladly regardless of rank, reputation or standing.

Albert was more than good enough so I hope you understand my immense pride.

The war was coming to a close, victory had been achieved, our freedom was secured. For Albert what next?

Life must go on, he was a married man with two young children, so, what next for this family breadwinner.

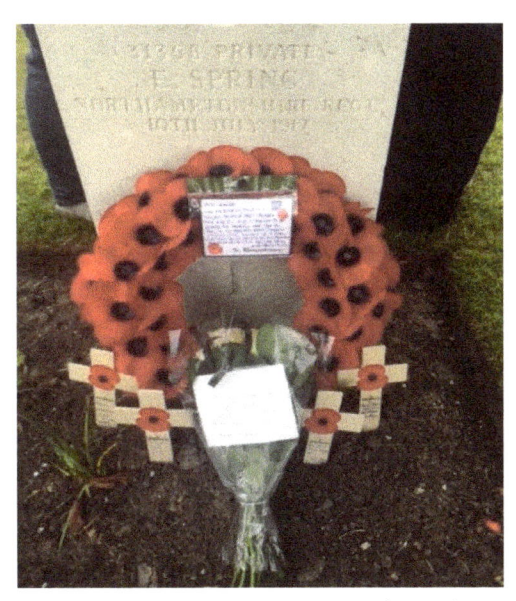

Grandad Spring's Grave on the 100th Anniversary
of his death on 10th July 1917

Dan & Phil paying their respects at Grandad
Spring's Grave on 10th July 2017

Our beautiful mum, Edith Olive Spring

The one and only Granny Farrer

Granny & Grampy Taylor, what can I say!

Albert Edward Spring: No Ordinary Man

Albert in Commando Training

Albert with his hard earnt Corporal's stripes!

In his Middle Eastern Commando gear including the pith helmet

Looks like Middle East 11th (Scottish) Commando outfit!

These are from authentic photos taken sometime during the war after the Litani River offensive in June 1941 with his handwritten comments below which were on the back.

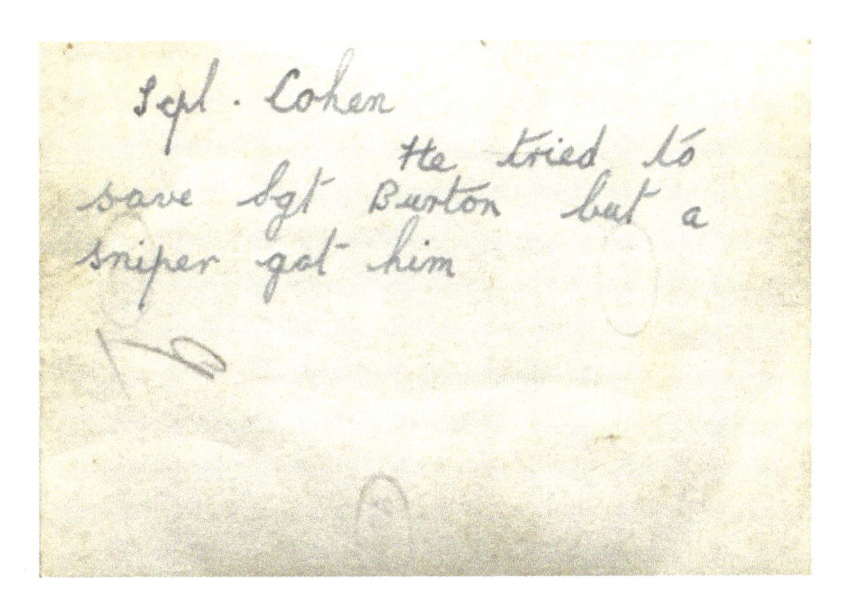

Cpl. Cohen
He tried to save Sgt Burton but a sniper got him

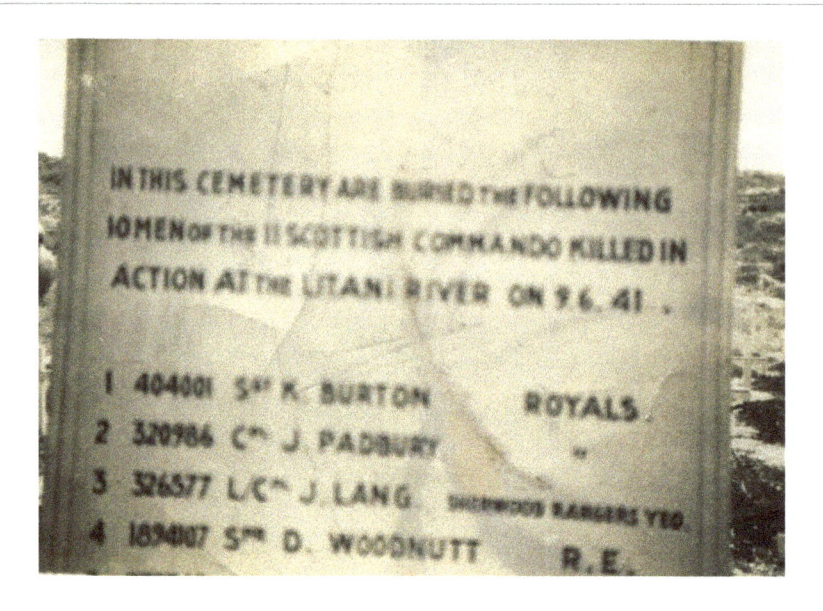

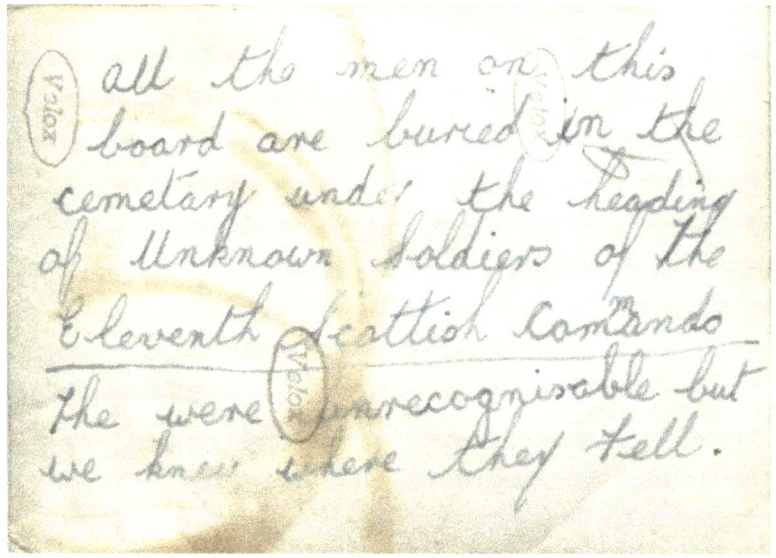

> IN THIS CEMETERY ARE BURIED THE FOLLOWING
> 10 MEN OF THE 11 SCOTTISH COMMANDO KILLED IN
> ACTION AT THE LITANI RIVER ON 9.6.41.
>
> 1 404001 S⁀ K. BURTON   ROYALS
> 2 320986 C⁀ J. PADBURY   "
> 3 326577 L/C⁀ J. LANG   SHERWOOD RANGERS YEO
> 4 1894007 S⁀ D. WOODNUTT   R.E.

> all the men on this board are buried in the cemetary under the heading of Unknown Soldiers of the Eleventh Scottish Comando. They were unrecognisable but we knew where they fell.

How poignant is that to think that could have been Albert because he was there in the heat of the battle

Ed Fulmer during the war

Johannes van Zanten

Fre de Jong in war time

Jim Westbury in uniform

Arnold Hayes from Rochdale

A random photo from the Middle East Commando Facebook page.
Albert is bottom right. Thank you MEC

2nd Battalion The Parachute Regiment marching through London on 17th September 1945. Sergeant Spring second from right on the front row

THE END OF THE WAR & DEMOB TIME

For a country boy Albert had always voted Conservative at the ballot box. However, when the General Election came in July 1945, after the war time coalition government, he voted Labour for the one and only time.

Why should he make such a strange switch? It was simple, the Labour Party promised all the servicemen they would be demobbed and be home with their families very quickly.

As Albert said, it was a no brainer. He and millions like him had had enough of war, it was time for peace and getting back to some form of normality.

Hence, Albert was demobbed in May 1946 after just over six years as a serving soldier.

His reward for doing so included a new suit, £60 and a job reference.

Hans Vervoorn could not believe it, given the Dutch government rewarded him with training him to be a Doctor. Albert's reward was much less, but he was going home to where he was the happiest, back in his beloved countryside of Huntingdonshire and perhaps back to a little poaching and more importantly a proper job that fed the family.

Albert should justifiably be proud of his contribution to this most important victory. I suspect he didn't see it that way. He saw it as simply doing his duty so let us not get too carried away.

AFTER THE WAR

So, what does a man do who's profession had been fighting and killing for the last five years or so? For Albert it was getting back to normal as best he could. As we know he was not a man of education having left school at the earliest opportunity resulting in most of his work being of a physical nature.

The one thing his war time experience gave him was physical fitness which allowed him to work long and hard. Hence, he found himself involved in building a new water tower in the local village of Hemington.

This was not simply building a water tower but all the infrastructure works such as pipelines that go with it to feed the local towns and villages. If I remember rightly, Dan told me Albert was a foreman on the job. In civilian parlance, this is a similar role to that of Sergeant in the army, where he was organising the men to get the work done. Hence a good fit for Albert, and it allowed him to earn a liveable wage although he never made money his God.

Dan tells me the tower is still there.

I am sure there would also have been a bit of poaching on the side because it was in his blood given he had been doing it since the age of seven!

On the home front, Dan and I arrived respectively in September 1947 and April 1949.

The family was getting bigger. Hence, it was time for their own home. After the war the government had embarked on a programme of building council houses as a means of improving the infrastructure for the returning forces and getting the economy going again after the war.

If you look around where you live you will find examples of such council house developments, even in the smallest of villages such as Winwick.

Six such properties were built up Thurning Road, three pairs of semis numbered 1 to 6 completed in the post year wars. Albert and Olive were allocated 1 Thurning Road as their new home with three bedrooms, one bathroom, a kitchen, scullery, larder and front room as we knew it plus a separate down stairs toilet and out houses including dad's barn. All good brick built buildings.

Number 1 has the largest garden and Dan and I think they were given that because of Albert's war time exploits.

Indeed he lived all his life in that very same house.

I am not sure how well Albert settled down to his so called normal life, but, with four young children there was plenty to keep him occupied.

Dan tells of incidents of fighting when some of his ex-army pals came to visit. After all, it must have taken some time to get the fighting thing out of the system.

POACHER TURNED GAMEKEEPER

By the late 1940s Albert was in his early thirties, hence, he was at the peak of physical condition. He was clearly a very good poacher who the local land owners simply could not catch.

One of the local land owners, believed to be Tom Parsons, who lived in a rather grand house in the village of Glatton, about six miles eastward on the B660 out towards the famous A1 road, had the bright idea to invite Albert to become his Gamekeeper working on the premise if you cannot catch them then employ them! Albert took to it with the same gusto and diligence he had demonstrated in his army career.

He was never short of work. As a Gamekeeper there is no such thing as nine til five for five days per week. It is a full time job, well, more of a vocation really as it required seven days per week, meaning it is seven days per week dawn til dusk, and sometimes even after dusk in to and during the night.

As an example of the fifty odd years he was officially a Gamekeeper mum and dad had one holiday away together and that was as a retirement present from his employers on the Hamerton Estate where he was keeper all that time.

At his official retirement event, held in Hamerton Village Hall, he declared he was leaving early because he didn't want to be late for work in the morning!

He was also involved in the Salome Wood estate out towards Leighton Bromswold which consisted of a nearby wood and farm land. Albert's heart was on the Hamerton estate, in the little village of Hamerton, of about three thousand acres of arable farm land with some woodland the main one of which was Hamerton Grove which was where Albert was at peace. Infact, his ashes are spread there in accordance with his last wishes.

This was to be Albert's life through the 1950s through to 2002 when he died.

He was a strict man who had clear principles of discipline and justice. We never wanted for much but then we didn't expect much anyway because we were taught to be self-sufficient.

As children, it was a matter of being seen and not heard. In the school summer holidays we were expected to get out of the house by no later than about 9.30 in the morning, come rain or shine, with instruction not to come back until tea time of 4.30 in the afternoon.

We were not hard done by, however, there was not a lot of love about, that's not to say we weren't loved but as in most families of the time it wasn't openly demonstrated. We just got on with life. We were expected to earn our pocket money and if you didn't do the allocated tasks of cutting the grass, cleaning the dogs pens or chopping the fire wood then you didn't get the money. I wonder how that would work in the modern day family today!

In all my fifty three years as his son, up to his death, I do not recall him once telling me he loved me. But that was how it was in those days. But what he, together with our mum, did do was instil in us a tremendous work ethic for which we are so grateful.

He developed his reputation as one of the finest Gamekeepers in the area. Perhaps, it is useful to explain what a keeper's role is.

It is a Gamekeeper's job to ensure enough game, pheasants or partridge, are available for a good days shooting with the resultant 'bag' on the eight to ten shooting days over the season from 1st October to 31st January. This is achieved by breeding additional pheasants and partridges and protecting them along with the existing stock from the various predators on the estate.

As usual, there is much more to this profession than meets the eye. Breeding game birds takes times, patience and very long hours and hard work. It is very similar to looking after typically 500 to 1,000 babies and as many of us know how hard it is to raise even one or two of them from birth.

Albert saw his role as protecting the weak and vulnerable from the strong (the predators). Every time I watch a David Attenborough nature programme I think of Albert. Nature, perhaps like life, is a tough world where it is all about the survival of the fittest.

Raising the game birds was one side of the job. Controlling the predators was another. Who are the predators? Foxes, weasels, badgers, cats, magpies and several other such birds or creatures of prey. Simply, they are any creature that will harm his beloved game birds and stop him delivering on shoot days.

There is a whole story here in its own right that is covered in two of the three books that Albert wrote namely 'Gamekeeping at Hamerton' and 'The Ways of the Wild' where Albert was a well-known source of knowledge. He also regularly contributed to the game shooting magazines of the day.

In his third book 'Characters' he talks about the different characters he came across in the best part of 86 years of his life. They include people and animals such as his dogs and badgers.

A tour of the contents of the garden at 1 Thurning Road would provide a good insight as to what was involved.

There were several kennels for the dogs, predominantly black and golden labradors as well as springer spaniel retrievers, and working terriers which went to ground to control foxes and badgers.

There was also a pen containing the ferrets which were used for catching rabbits. Those damn ferrets could really bite and it was not easy to release the lock of their jaws on your finger. That brings back one or two painful memories! There was nothing finer in his world for Albert than to spend a day rabbiting with his pal Jimmy Turner from the next village of Great Gidding. It was also a good way of generating additional income by selling the catch to the local butchers.

Rabbits, pheasants and pigeons were a source of food for the family and the community. These are seen as delicacies and treats these days. However, when you are the son of a Gamekeeper you are sick to the back teeth of them and never want to eat them again!

It is important to remember, in those days, there was not the convenience shopping of super markets and the likes that we enjoy today.

Our retail world consisted of Bocky Foster, the mobile butcher, Eric and Dawn Hoskins & Tony Garner, the mobile grocers, with fish and chips hopefully on a Friday evening. Also there was no going on line to sort your insurance; it was simply the man from the Pru coming round once per month to collect the premiums. Our clothes came from the J D Williams catalogue delivered all the way from Manchester which seemed a life time away. I always smile when I see their advertisements either on line or on the television as they are still going to this day.

Dan also reminded me of the various other travelling shops and specialist suppliers such as Billy Yeomans, our Post man, who could turn his hand to anything and would help out in any way he could. That was how it was in those days; everybody knew everybody else and would help each other without seeking a reward.

Albert also had a very large garden. He was a great gardener because in those days you needed to be self-sufficient in putting food on the table. Four hungry boys take some feeding at the most economical price.

Hence, he grew his own vegetables. Not only did he put food on our demanding table but on the table of many others in the village and his friends from the surrounding villages.

The highlight of the week or indeed the month was a trip to the local towns of Peterborough (13 miles away) and Huntingdon (8 miles away). There were two buses per week; one on a Saturday and one on a Wednesday where the locals could enjoy the pleasures of town life for three or four hours before their return. There was the luxury of a Woolworths, a Marks & Spencer or Brierley's in Peterborough. My Granny Farrer loved a visit to Frank Brierley's famous discount store just over the bridge in Peterborough or to see her sister Ginny who also lived off Lincoln Road.

Effectively, Albert was his own boss hence this is a world so far removed from his wartime time exploits ranging from Scotland, England, South Africa, Egypt, North Africa, Palestine, Lebanon, Cyprus , the Mediterranean, Italy and the Netherlands!

There were no obvious signs of any PTSD (Post Traumatic Stress Disorder) which we know and hear so much more about these days. It is important to remember at that time to show any form of stress or mental health problems was seen as weakness. Therefore, most people hid or supressed it and got on with life as best as they could hoping time would be the healer.

However, the war must have had a considerable impact upon him. It must have done; no body or soul could have endured what he had encountered without a significant impact upon him.

As before he was a strict man, he could shout and was quick of temper. You certainly did not want to get the wrong side of Albert Spring!

Whilst it was not an openly loving relationship, it did us no harm. It certainly taught us to stand up for ourselves.

The one enemy of being a Gamekeeper, I have not mentioned, is the poacher, who was keen to steal the Keeper's beloved birds by whatever means possible including violence, if necessary.

There was a constant tussle; a constant battle of the wits.

You didn't mess with Albert. As an example, one fool hardy poacher decided he was going to teach Albert a lesson by giving him a good hiding by cutting him up whilst Albert and Olive were driving over to Sawtry to visit friends one evening in the family van when Albert was in his 60s.

Mum described the incident where this car came from behind at speed and swerved across the front of their path blocking the way. The angry man jumped out and started abusing Albert, who immediately got out of the van. The next thing was the veteran dumped the poacher in to the adjacent ditch with a few strategically placed blows. It was all over in a few moments. The aggressor was vanquished in the bottom of the soggy wet ditch.

Albert calmly got back in the van, started the engine and pulled out and continued with their journey. All he said was "that will teach him to mess with a man trained by the SAS." This was him at his boastful best.

He was a man of action and not words.

He had a number of close friends such as Jimmy Turner, Jim Edwards, Mervyn and his brother Tom Joyce, Malcolm Houghton and Oscar Jordan. They were very strong relationships and he was never happier than when he was in their company with the odd glass of whisky. This was long before the days of the drink driving campaign and subsequent legislation.

He was involved with the local British Legion; I remember him being the standard bearer in the local churches on Remembrance Day. Having attended a few of those, not for one minute, did I dream I would be writing a book about it all these years later. He was a well respected member of the community. He was the go to man and he certainly kept his council.

There is a memorial stone in Winwick church noting Albert as one of the few men of this small village that served their country in World War II.

Occasionally, he would go off to reunions of the 10th Battalion The Parachute Regiment in Melton Mowbray which is close to Somerby. He was going back to remember his war times there and perhaps, more importantly, to remember his fallen comrades and share the fellowship of his fellow veterans.

It came to light that because of what happened on the fateful day of Monday 18th September 1944 Albert was awarded an honorary membership of the USAF 315th Troop Carrier Group at their invitation. Whilst I know very little about this, I understand that Albert was known to be their guest at one of their reunions in London. He would have enjoyed that although he certainly kept it quiet. He was no braggart.

In going through his papers after his passing in 2002, we saw it there in writing for the first time, as to his part in those very brave airmen receiving their richly deserved bravery awards.

LOSING OUR MUM

1989 was not a good year, although it contained my fortieth birthday. Our mum had been struggling health wise although she was only in her early seventies.

After not being well for some time she was admitted to Hinchingbrooke Hospital Huntingdon where I certainly had not realised the severity of her health issues. Given I had lived up in the north west since the early 1970s, which is about a three hour drive away, I still made sure we visited mum in hospital.

The big C had struck again, mum was seriously ill with Cancer, to which she succumbed and, sadly, passed away on the evening of Sunday 17th September 1989 in hospital at the age of 72.

This was an extremely sad time for us all. Everyone was there except Arthur. He did not like hospitals and was reluctant to go to visit even his own mum on her deathbed. Fair play to him though, he did come to see her and, would you believe, she made more fuss of him than any of us. She was so pleased to see him that Saturday for just an hour or so. Now, contented mum was at peace and passed away at about 8 o'clock on the following evening.

I started to cry and my Dad put his hand on my shoulder and said, "don't cry son, if you have seen as many people die or be killed as I have then you realise life is cheap and there is no point in being sad." I suppose this was father's coping mechanism kicking in.

One of his mantras was 'never be sad at a funeral'. He went on to say always think of the good times you enjoyed with that person. Otherwise, it will bring you down. That is good advice which, I have always tried to adopt.

I had never seen anybody die before and had been warned that I would find it difficult not only at the time but in the weeks afterwards. That advice was absolutely bang on. I did struggle with it, having no mum was so strange, maybe it is the final cutting of the umbilical cord.

Coincidentally, and perhaps bizarrely, our mum died 45 years to the day after the first day of the battle of Arnhem.

Mother's funeral was held at Kettering crematorium and it was a rather a solemn affair attended by all the country folk who knew her and our family.

Upon reflection, I wish we, her sons and me in particular, had done more to celebrate her life and give her the send-off she richly deserved.

Life had been tough for this wonderful lady living in a testosterone filled world of five men. As I have said, there was not a lot of love and affection involved. There was more rough and tumble of a man's world where hurting each other's feelings or giving each other a thump was not an issue. If only we had been more compassionate towards her. Like most things in life you only really appreciate what you have when it is gone.

Mother had run the household with very little support and domestic help from her husband or us boys. She was also a hard worker. Much of Dan and my summer school holidays were spent potato picking in Ian Carr's fields in Hamerton come rain or shine. Our mum was the potato picking queen of all time; picking one hundred bags from 9.30 to 3.30 was not a problem aided and abetted by us two school boys who could be prone to adding in the odd stone or two to make up the numbers.

Olive was a very well respected worker who would deliver a whole field of sugar beet hoeing to the highest standard on her own with a little help from Dan and me.

Gamekeepers did not earn much money so as you can appreciate the finances were very tight and life could be frugal. But mum managed the best she could with not a great deal of financial or moral support.

Such a life took its toll hence we lost our anchor at a much earlier age than she deserved.

Given my son, James and his wife Olivia have four children spread over a similar age range, I realise now how hard it must have been for mum and indeed father all those years ago.

Our mum, alongside so many other such wives and partners, was one of those forgotten heroes from those very difficult and testing times.

RETURNING TO ARNHEM

After losing our mum the inevitable question was how would father cope; would he quickly pass on without his all-important crutch of over fifty years or would he find a new way forward?

He took the latter course which, on reflection was again most probable, given his fiercely independent nature and life experiences he had ploughed through as a result of losing his own father at such a young age and then his war experiences.

He learned how to feed and look after himself. He was an excellent record keeper all in his own scrawly hand writing. There were no lap tops or computers in those days; it was all done in long hand.

Given his standing as a first class Gamekeeper he was invited to write articles for various shooting magazines.

Sitting in the front room, he wrote long hand written manuscripts for his three books which were subsequently printed and published.

He also wrote the story about the village of Winwick where he had lived all his life. I must still have the manuscript somewhere which will be worth looking at when I retire!

The story of whether or not to publish his first book 'Gamekeeping at Hamerton' was interesting. He rarely asked us boys for advice on anything. However, he was indecisive about paying six thousand pounds to publish it or not. He asked me what I thought to which I replied have you got the money to which he said yes. I replied it is a no brainer then. Whether that was the affirmation or not he was looking for he went ahead and published it.

Unbeknown to me Albert was being sought out to go back to Arnhem by the very same Hans Vervoorn who had saved his life back in 1944.

As a result there was an invitation on the table to go and spend time with Hans and his family in Holland (or should I say the Netherlands) to retrace his steps from all those years before. We, his sons and his wider family, knew very little about what had happened because it did not get talked about.

Bearing in mind he was approaching his seventy fifth birthday on the 6th May 1991 the usual indecision in such matters was back. So in the February of 1991 I visited my dad for one of our not so highly communicable exchanges. I do not know whether it was his pride that refused to allow him to ask me to take him back or whether he was simply unsure. I suspect the former.

Anyway I said, "look father if you want to go back I will organise the trip and I will take you." Hesitantly he said "yes", hence we were going.

Arrangements were made and we were booked on the ferry from Harwich to the Hook of Holland in early May 1991 for a ten day stay in Amersfoort in the Netherlands with Hans and Wil Vervoorn. The last time Albert and Hans had been together was on 23rd September 1944 in Boven Leeuwen after they had crossed the River Waal at night. It was the best part of 47 years since the last time they had been in each other's company!

Come the day, with me living up in the north west, I picked up Albert in the afternoon on the way to the ferry port of Harwich towards the bottom end of the bulge of East Anglia.

We had sorted all our gifts, those wreaths, the red beret and the medals as well as the bags packed plus our all-important foreign currency.

We were on the overnight ferry to the Hook of Holland. We enjoyed a good meal before turning in for the night in our cabin.

For those of you who use the overnight ferry, you do not get a full night's sleep because with the time difference between Europe and the UK you are awakened at about 5.30 am so you are lucky to get six or seven hours sleep at best.

I always struggle with this arrangement because I know I have got to be up early so my built in alarm clock doesn't let me sleep properly anyway.

Regardless, we were up and ready to go even at this unearthly hour.

In the lead up to our visit I had studied the map of the Netherlands and had worked out our best route to Amersfoort where Hans and Wil lived. I cannot remember if I had a Satnav or not but just in case I more than likely had also prepared a written list of our route just like we used to do before we had the luxury of such electronic gadgets.

Looking at the map, I estimated it would be about a three hour journey so our hosts could expect us about eleven or eleven thirty, assuming we would be off the ferry about eight or eight thirty at the latest.

Wrongly, I had assumed the Netherlands was about the same geographical size as the UK. It was a school boy error because we arrived about ninety minutes early.

Regardless, without too many wrong turns, we arrived at Hans and Wil's beautiful home in Amersfoort.

Neither Albert nor I were sure what to expect as we did not have the details of the itinerary for the ten days with them. It simply did not matter.

We were made to feel very welcome and Albert was given the best bedroom because he was the guest of honour. The house was three storeys with my bedroom being on the top floor.

We enjoyed a typical Dutch breakfast with plenty of cheese if I remember correctly.

Despite the passage of time the respect shown between these two remarkable men was obvious.

Hans explained the programme of events. There was going to be two Burgemeesters receptions for this returning hero. Father was somewhat perplexed because he did not see himself that way; he thought their presence at the battle had only brought the Dutch people trouble. Hans explained the Paras brought them hope of their liberation from the Nazi tyranny and their ultimate freedom.

Regarding their liberation, there are two significant days in the Dutch calendar; the first one being their Remembrance Day or should I say evening on the 4th May and their World War II Liberation Day the next day on 5th May. Hans went off to show his respect although we didn't really understand how it all worked at this point.

The 6th May 1991 was a significant day too as it was Albert's 75th birthday. The Dutch did not fail; they came up with a makeshift 75th birthday card, at such short notice, made out to Sergeant Albert Spring depicting him parachuting on to Dutch soil. I am proud to say still have original in my house!

The Burgemeesters' receptions were something else. There was typical Dutch hospitality with coffee and biscuits, there were speeches and presentations; some we understood and some we didn't, most of all there were people from back the last time they had been together in 1944 when Albert was in his army gear rather than civilian clothes. He, like me, wasn't quite sure what to make of it all but he did come up with the goods when saying a few words in response.

Unlike last time there were no guns, no fighting or fear. There was only respect and admiration for their returning hero. They had clearly been planning this for some time and, on this occasion, their reluctant hero had obliged.

As well as Hans, there was Fre de Jong and Harry Tomeson who were both veterans of those few days all those years ago. I wondered what must have been going through their heads!

We were taken to Kesteren to the grave of Johannes van Zanten which is very impressive. Albert paid his deepest respects to a man he totally respected even after all these years.

This was also the opportunity to meet the van Zanten family who treated my father and me so well. We will never forget their care and love towards Albert. Remember, father and his fellow Paras represented trouble for their family and it could be said they played their part in the death of their father.

And to think we had not even got to Arnhem yet to visit the cemetery at Oosterbeek so plans were afoot. I suggested to Hans he should join us for our visit along with the intended drop zone site at Ginkel Heath on the way. He said, "no you go on your own as you will understand why."

So off we went, firstly to Ginkel Heath, which is exactly that, a large heath land ideal for a large parachute drop surrounded by trees albeit about eleven kilometres from the intended target of the bridge in the centre of Arnhem. So much for a surprise attack!

In writing this it brings back to my mind's eye those photos of the Germans shooting the Paras as they dropped out of the sky.

Then on to the cemetery to find the grave of Alfred Penwill and for father to, at long last, be at peace knowing his friends final resting place.

There was much more to see than that. I shall never forget watching him walk along the rows of gravestones and as before telling me about his involvement with each of them. It was like he was talking about his mates but it was a bit more serious than that.

It was very emotional when we found the grave of Alfred. Again as before peace of mind for Albert at long last.

After Penwill we found the graves of Kenneth Smyth, Bill Burgess, Doc Drayson (as Albert called him) and, of course, Lionel Queripel.

As we stood at Drayson's grave Albert told me how he had been killed by a stray bullet whilst he was treating wounded soldiers from both sides in what is now the Hartenstein Airborne Museum, which was a field hospital then. Isn't that a bizarre end for a man and officer father highly respected!

Indeed the whole experience was so emotional, particularly given we did not know what to expect.

Albert and I had done our duty so we returned to Hans and Wil feeling pleased and proud with what we had achieved that day.

On another day this time with Hans and Wil and many others we also visited the brick factory and the crossing point of the River Waal where they embarked for that intrepid crossing in the middle of the night. We visited the property where the soldiers had been delivered to for their freedom.

There was the chance to get to know the families of the Vervoorns, the van Zantens, the de Jongs and the Tomesons.

We were given a tour of the site where Ed Fulmer had managed to crash land his Dakota. Father was presented with two pieces of the shrapnel from their very plane by a local historian who's name I wish I could remember.

Along with a visit to the all-important Hazenhof, which was the Paras home for those three or four days way back then, to stand on the very spot where the farmer had produced the paperwork to prove his daughter had died the previous evening of diphtheria. If only the Germans had known the truth!

We were made so welcome by the current owners Jan and Sophie van Velzen. These two wonderful people had embraced the history of this important landmark property.

Jan and Sophie became special friends. It was always so important to visit them including up to September 2022 when we last saw Jan before he passed. Tremendous people who will be remembered forever. They looked after father and all those involved by treating them so well.

We were also blessed with the opportunity to meet with and share such good times with the children of Johannes van Zanten namely, in order of the eldest first, Dirk (the speed skater), Jan (the shooting man), Jannie, Irene and last but not least, Wim (the motor bike racer). Sadly only Irene is still with us. Excellent people nonetheless. Albert enjoyed their company very much and I even have a photo of him presenting the parachute wings to Wim's young daughter as a child, who now has a family of her own. How time flies!

We did not know it at the time but we were making long term deep friendships forged from the deeds of these special people all those years before.

I am so proud to say those friendships continue to this day with the likes of Lieke, Majorke and Hans junior Vervoorn; Irene and Arjen de Jong. No doubt I have missed a number of names to whom I apologise for my poor memory.

This was the beginning of something very special including the forging of the bonds between our respective families and long may it continue.

I saw my dad in a totally different light as a result of these few days. I knew he had been involved with the war effort with the Commandos and the Paras. But I did not know he was a hero; he never told us that all important bit!

Wow, this was my dad. I was forty two years of age and this was a life changing occasion. I now saw Albert in a different light. Again he was the master of the understatement.

We returned back to the ferry after a wonderful experience on Dutch soil. Life had changed for ever.

Once on the ferry, it was time to think about gifts for the people back home. I thought Albert was going to buy up the whole gift shop! Everybody back home got something with some getting two gifts. I don't think I had ever seen him so happy. The visit had meant a great deal to him and he was delighted he had made the effort.

I mentioned earlier Albert never made money his king. When we were on our way home he said to me "I don't want you to be out of pocket" as he gave me one hundred pounds to cover my costs. They certainly don't make them like Albert anymore.

MEETING ED FULMER & FURTHER VISITS

This was the beginning of a journey of several visits back to those places including the fiftieth anniversary of the liberation of the Netherlands in May 1995 where we met Ed and Lucille Fulmer for the first time.

Again, it was an honour to be sharing the company of a Knight of the Dutch realm. A man who had displayed such bravery in the worst of adversity. It was an honour and a privilege to share his company.

He reminded me very much of Albert as he was very understated and very unassuming. And yet, he was a true hero who enjoyed lunch with the Queen of the Netherlands and then was out for a beer with us later that very same day. What an experience! We even had to make him wear his hard earned and richly deserved medals.

On one of our visits we were in the town of Arnhem. Both Jim Westbury and Albert were wearing their Parachute Regiment Association blazers and their red berets. I popped into a shop and when I returned they both stood there looking rather perplexed. They told me the story of this lady coming along and thanking them for all they did at Arnhem and presenting them with a bar of soap each. These two tough veterans were genuinely touched by this wonderful gesture.

On one of the visits to the cemetery father mentioned the name of Denzil Keen, a Para who father knew way back then. Albert wanted to know what had become of him because he was of the Jewish religion and insisted on wearing the Star of David, against Albert's advice, rather than the standard identity dog tags.

Keen had dropped on Ginkel Heath alongside his pal who broke his leg. His pal was taken prisoner and Denzil was never seen again. Albert had remembered him after all this time.

Given the issues with discipline with the Paras I asked him how they controlled the inevitable conflicts and discipline on a day to day basis. Albert said that was simple, everywhere they went they took boxing gloves with them.

If there was friction or a fall out they, the Company, formed a human boxing ring, and those in conflict sorted it out man to man. That is how father had come across Denzil Keen. He said they even had the gloves with them on the plane at Arnhem but, sadly, they burned with Chalk Mark 697!

We enjoyed many a special time with Hans and Wil. One poignant moment comes to mind when Hans took us to a rather large unkempt cemetery near to Amersfoort where he asked if we knew anything about it, which we didn't. Hans explained this was a cemetery full of Russian soldiers who had been transferred to the Netherlands for whatever reason and, sadly, they had caught influenza, which killed them before a bullet was fired in anger.

How sad is that and I suspect nobody bothers too much about it.

Going back to Arnhem through the 1990s gave the opportunity for us Spring boys, with the usual exemption of Arthur, to go back there together. On one occasion Dan drove us everywhere. Thanks Dan.

On another occasion I can recall Hans, Wil, Albert and I took a chain ferry crossing in the Dutch countryside to finish up standing on a bridge over a canal in what seemed like the middle of nowhere. Hans, with a cheeky smile on his face, told us how he and Fre and Harry used an enclosed truck disguised as an ambulance including the obligatory red cross signs to steal and transport what they had stolen from the various Dutch Post Offices.

They decided to steal them and break them open in some remote quiet spot because their previous attempts to break them open insitu had proven disastrous because they had used too much explosive resulting in destroying the whole safe including the much coveted ration cards which they need to obtain food rations for the Allied service men they had hidden away behind enemy lines.

As we stood on this particular bridge Hans told us, in that cool calm manner of his, how in the middle of the night he and his erstwhile colleagues would bring the opened safes in their so called ambulance in the middle of the night and throw them over the side into the water below, with their secret submerged and hopefully lost forever!

They were young, brave with a definite cause therefore the consequences of getting caught did not seem to cross their minds way back then.

I can recall at the time of looking at Hans and thinking you did what! I dread to think what the enemy would have done to them and their fellow country folk. I don't think it would have been a matter of a fair trial do you?

Hans and Wil came to visit Albert and us his family. Hans spoke at the fiftieth Tenth Battalion reunion dinner. They stayed with Albert at 1 Thurning Road in his house as they wanted to understand and share their hero's way of life.

For Albert's 80th birthday in 1996 we arranged for him to visit Ed and Lucille at their home in Syracuse in New York State of the United States of America.

What a way for these two unique people, both heroes in their own right, to spend valuable time together again.

Ironically, this was the first time that we saw signs of Albert's health issues. Liz Spring, who accompanied him on the visit, said she had been really worried about him because as we know being reasonably fit and healthy is important when travelling and he struggled from thereon.

Having said that there was another fine example of his dry sense of humour. On the flight back he sat next to two American ladies who loved meeting an English gentleman.

They asked what he thought of their beloved country. Albert replied "well everything is so big. The houses are big, the gardens are big, there are big wide open spaces in this big country, the portions of food are so big I could not eat it all and of course the women are so big." I don't think they spoke to him again for the rest of the flight!

That is what made Albert so unique. He was one on his own. He was his own man who told you how it was like it or not!

The last time I took him back to Holland was in 1999 and, like taking the bridge at Arnhem, it was a trip too far. He was really struggling with his breathing; his lungs were failing him. We took an electric wheel chair and oxygen to help him breathe. He coped but he was clearly failing. I will always remember how Wil Vervoorn and Irene Bruning van Zanten looked after and cared for this old gentleman.

On the ferry coming home I was most concerned whether he was going to make it. Thankfully he did and he was home safely. However, alas, he would never return to the Netherlands.

What saddened me the most was seeing this man who had been one of the fittest men in the county decline. I cannot help but think of him on the front row marching through London as a member of one of the finest fighting forces in the world. Simply so proud, so strong and totally invincible.

He had been a stalwart to his country, his family, his friends and his community. More importantly, he did not expect much, if anything, in return. Money was not his God. He was never happier than when he was out in the countryside either walking or hunting with one of his dogs or his close friends.

Hans Vervoorn, Jim Westbury & Albert Spring reunited
after the best part of 47 years

Our wonderful hosts Hans &
Wil Vervoorn

Hans & Albert, old friends
since 1944!

Burgemeesters Reception
1991 for the returning hero

Harry and Albert meet again since the last time in 1944

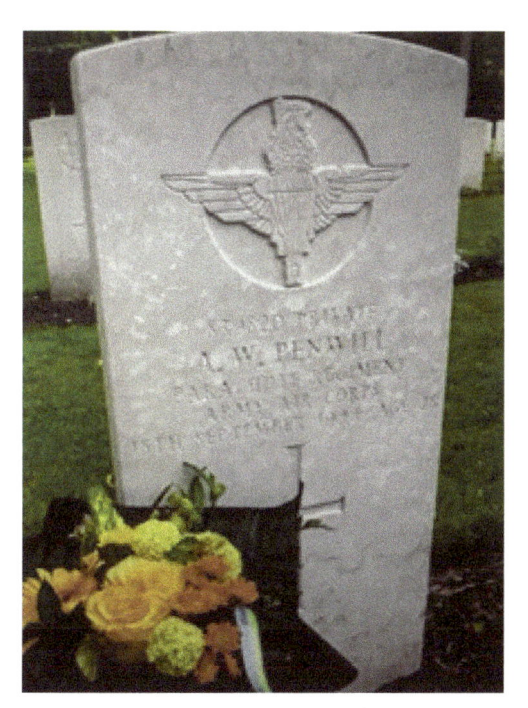

Peace at last Alfred Penwill's grave
with flowers

Albert Edward Spring: No Ordinary Man

Fre & Albert together again reflecting from all those years ago

The Kangaroo & Albert meet again

Johannes van Zanten's grave in
Kesteren

The Dutch marking Albert's 75th Birthday –
Rather Special

Aircraft Chalk Mark 697 1944 crash & drop zone site in 1991

Two veteran Paras reflecting on their memories in that very same field in September 1944

Two very special ladies Wil Vervoorn & Irene Bruning van Zanten
Their caring and respect for Albert was truly remarkable

More of the Burgermeester's reception with a young
Arjen de Jong

With two more rather special friends namely Jan & Sophie van Velzen at the Hazenhof

The Vervoorn and Spring families starting to form that unique bond!

Jim Westbury, Ed Fulmer, Albert and Hans, four of our heroes back together again. What a moment!

The resplendent Hazenhof in Kesteren. The home of the Paras behind enemy lines in September 1944

Lucille, Albert, Fre and Jim standing up with Ed and Hans in front ready for the unveiling of the plaque at the Hazenhof

Albert, Jim and Ed admiring the plaque on the wall at the Hazenhof

Edward Simons Fulmer wearing his much deserved Knight of
the Military Order of Willam. A reluctant but real hero

Hans Vervoorn, also wearing his Bronze Lion bravery
award and medals. Another true unassuming super hero

Father and son, Albert and Phil when we met Ed Fulmer for the very first time in 1995

Albert saying a few words at the Hazenhof including him wearing his red beret

Jim Westbury in civvies. He and his daughter Rona joined us on several occasions in Holland

Reg Shurbourne also in civvies. A true gentleman who thought his world was ending as he stood ready to jump!

Jim and Reg were big pals as soldiers and afterwards

Albert and Ed enjoying time together at Ed and Lucille's home in Syracuse USA in 1996

10th Battalion The Parachute Regiment RSM

"Chalkie" White.

A professional solder and later a Chelsea Pensioner

He was so proud of his men!

Albert and Hans plotting!

Wil, Rona, Albert, Hans and Jim with Nellie Zilstra, the young girl who sang the song when the Germans came

More discussions with Ed & Lucille Fulmer
when they met in May 1995

Every 4th May in Kesteren there is a remembrance service at and flowers laid on the grave of Johannes van Zanten.

Now that is respect

A group photo outside Kesteren Town Hall in maybe 2019. So many friends together

Tilly's Three Wise Monkeys Dan, Phil and James!

Albert Edward Spring: No Ordinary Man

THE TENTH
1942 — 1945

X
BATTALION
THE PARACHUTE REGIMENT
FIFTIETH ANNIVERSARY
REUNION
DINNER AND DANCE

HELD AT
THE LEICESTERSHIRE
MOAT HOUSE
SATURDAY 11th APRIL 1992

The 50th anniversary Reunion Dinner and Dance of the 10th Battalion

Hans Vervoorn and Albert were there!

The veterans and our heroes enjoying getting together again.

There was a tale or two to be told!

Albert with his veteran Para friends at his surprise 80th birthday party in Winwick Village Hall in 1996

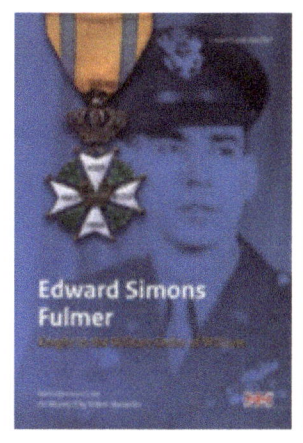

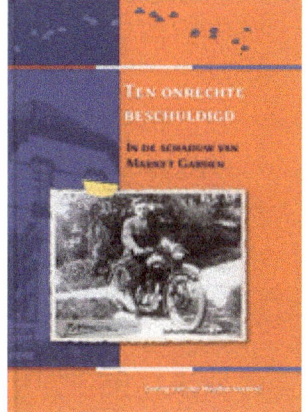

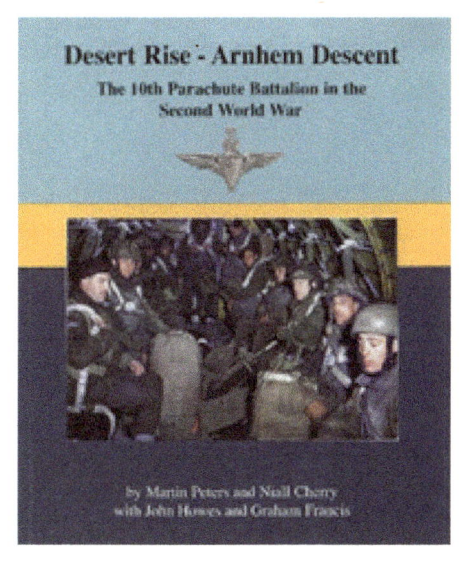

All I wanted was to see my dad's name, Albert Spring, written in a book about the war.

Would you believe he gets a mention in all seven.

He must have been a little more than an ordinary man!

What a collection. Thank you one and all

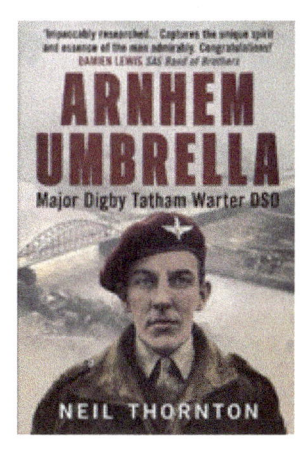

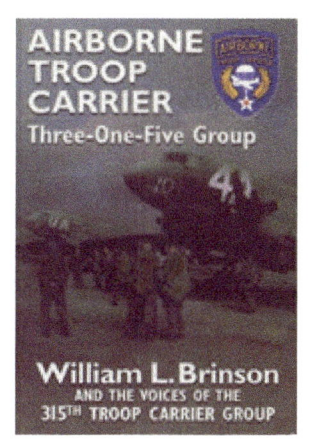

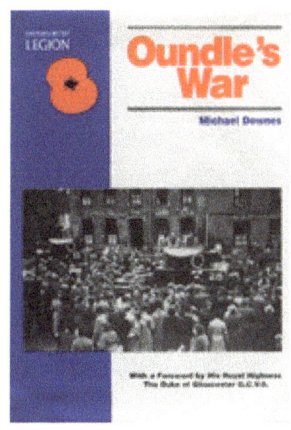

THE REMAINING YEARS

Albert struggled with his health but he was still relatively active and independent although my brother Dan and sister in law Marie would not necessarily agree because he became more demanding in those final few years. He needed to be taken here or there. He wanted something done and he wanted it done there and then!

In those latter years, because of his health issues, the local community services got involved as they felt it important, given he lived on his own, they check him out daily. A community nurse / health visitor was assigned to visit him every morning to check he was up and was looking after himself.

Albert had not had anybody checking up on him throughout his whole life so it wasn't going to be easy.

There were occasions where he would simply leave a note for his Carer that said, "Gone out, however there is water in kettle and there is milk and sugar so make yourself a cup of tea." He was still fiercely independent!

He got at odds with the local community services because they saw it as their duty, indeed their mandate, to check up on Albert and, paradoxically, charge him for the pleasure.

Albert did not take too kindly to this because of where he had come from through history. He had experienced the new era after the war, the birth of the National Health Service and the promise of free healthcare from the cradle to the grave.

Therefore, he did not take kindly to receiving a bill for this caring service he had never asked for in the first place. He reminded them of the promise of free care from the cradle to the grave on more than one occasion. It was a point of principle.

I got wind of this dispute, hence, got involved by promising to underwrite the bill behind his back so to speak. However true to form father reluctantly settled the bill through gritted teeth.

He still received visits from his friends where they enjoyed a good old chin wag over a cup of tea and a biscuit in the kitchen as before.

As time passed by he was becoming increasingly frustrated with his health issues and he was slowly losing his enthusiasm for life. Dan says father died of frustration which, on reflection, is true.

For Albert it was about the quality of life not the quantity. I am not sure how he would deal with the current issues of dementia and the like. Thankfully, he was still reasonably compos mentis to the very end.

Seeing him with an oxygen mask was not the real Albert. He had lost his independence and he simply did not like it. In a nutshell, it was not the way he wanted to live.

LOSING ALBERT

He was taken into Hinchingbrooke Hospital in Huntingdon, the very same hospital where Olive had lost her fight for life some thirteen years earlier.

None of us siblings were sure how long he would last, it was simply down to his will to live.

Knowing father was not in good order I travelled down to see him on the Wednesday 24th April 2002, the day before my birthday. He was losing the will to live which he approached in his usual pragmatic manner. My daughter Emma suggested I take him a new warm fleece we had just bought for work. When I gave it to him he said, "don't take it out of the bag because where I am going I will not need that." As I say, practical as ever right to the end.

That was the last time I saw him, and to be honest, we shared a few awkward silent moments before I returned back up north.

On the evening of Friday 26th April 2002 at about 8.00 pm Dan called me from the hospital car park to say father was asleep when he had just visited. Then a few minutes later my mobile goes again. It is Dan to say the hospital had just called him to say Albert had died in his sleep.

I am not a naturally emotional person but I just burst into tears, I could not stop crying, I was overcome by emotion. It was like the end of an era. Although I was expecting it I was not ready for it. My rock had gone forever, both my parents were no longer here.

Rather coincidentally and spookily Hans Vervoorn's birthday is also on that very same day 26th April. How do you explain that? Again an inexplicable coincidence or bond!

We, as a family were shell shocked at losing our Patriarch. He had been the leader of our family from when he was seven years old back in 1923 through to his death in 2002. That is the best part of eighty years as the leader of a family that went through the usual challenges plus the added burden of going through a World War.

This was certainly the end of an era for the Spring family.

It took the weekend to inform every one of our loss and, more importantly, for us four boys to come to terms with our loss and what we had to do next.

So at the beginning of the week we set about registering his death which Dan and I duly did at the Registry office in Huntingdon.

We also started going through Albert's papers just like any other family does at such a time. We were not the first and will not be the last!

Naturally, we had informed Hans Vervoorn of losing Albert. Again another irony because the last time Albert and I were in the Netherlands Hans took me to one side and made it very clear I was to inform him immediately if anything happened to father. With him being a Doctor he could see the writing was on the wall.

I kept my promise and Hans was duly informed. I thought I had made it clear we would be making arrangements once the weekend was over and the relevant parties for the funeral arrangements were back at work.

Having said that, I got this call from Hans early that week saying he and Wil were already in the UK ready for the funeral!

What does one do in such a situation? So on our way to see them, at their hotel between Huntingdon and Cambridge, Dan and I came up with a plan. We decided we would take them to see Albert in the morgue.

We dutifully explained the arrangements here in England take a little longer than perhaps in the Netherlands. Hans and Wil felt very privileged to have been able to be able to pay their last respects and goodbyes to their dear friend. For Hans he had lost one of his super heroes who he had met in that field the best part of sixty years previously.

We packed off Hans and Wil to catch the ferry back to their home country to return once the arrangements had been finalised.

THE FUNERAL

So we set about making the arrangements for the funeral for our dad, our hero.

Like most things in life nothing is as straight forward as expected albeit Albert wanted a simple cremation service. He did not want a church service. He was not a particularly religious person.

We had to think about the military side of his life which needed to be considered. The one aspect to be greatly admired about the military family and the Parachute Regiment in particular was their response to losing one of their beloved veterans. I can remember calling the standard bearer for the Parachute Regiment Association to tell him our sad news and he said so succinctly "let us know when and where it is and we will be there." That is how much they revered and remembered their veterans. The ultimate sign of respect.

The arrangements were made for Albert's send off at the crematorium in Kettering on Wednesday 8th May 2002, two days after his 86th birthday, for a relatively straight forward service.

Hans and Wil Vervoorn were back as they were not going to miss the funeral of their dear friend. Hans had asked to speak at the funeral.

When the day came there was an excellent turn out. That is a total understatement because the crematorium was packed and spilt over to outside with standing room only. We estimated it to be over 400 paying their last respects to this highly respected figure.

The Parachute Regiment Association and the British Legion were there in force with their standards.

Mike Alderman, Albert's and Olive's long term neighbour, said the airborne prayer. Albert's local Vicar, Canon Girard, lead the service.

Michael Halford, a long term family farmer friend from Grange Farm Hamerton, summed it all up when he wrote in the Hamerton Village magazine "if you had been at Kettering Crematorium the other day you would have thought it was the funeral of a member of the Royal family or a past Prime Minister. But no, it was only Albert's funeral."

That sums up the total respect for and the standing of Albert. He would have dismissed it all as unnecessary and undeserved. For once, he would have had to eat humble pie because his friends, the local people and those who knew him best had spoken by turning out in their droves.

When it was Albert's 80th birthday in 1986 we arranged a surprise party for him and his family and friends in Winwick village hall. Everybody was gathered there in expectation. The only two people missing were Albert and me, because he was adamant he wasn't going because nobody had told him about it in advance! A bit of a dilemma for a surprise birthday party, therefore I put it to him straight, "you are either coming now or we will have the party without you."

He was the guest of honour and he thoroughly enjoyed the celebrations with his family, friends and fellow veterans from the Parachute Regiment. He enjoyed it that much that he said when he died he wanted something similar for his wake.

Therefore, following the service at the crematorium we held his wake at the Mill at Barnwell with the best part of two hundred in attendance to celebrate this remarkable man's life, with all the catering organised by his granddaughter Lisa and her husband Neil.

This was the opportunity to remember this truly outstanding man.

Hans Vervoorn spoke of his feelings towards, regard and respect for Albert, his friend and his hero. I honestly think he thought Albert was ten feet tall, having two heads and spoke of him being a proper man.

Michael Halford, the dear friend, spoke of his time with Albert. It is important to remember farmers and Albert did not always see eye to eye! Michael told the wonderful story of father arriving up at Michael's home at Grange Farm Hamerton to find the family dog with a dead chicken tied round its neck. Albert immediately reproached Michael by saying "sir, why has that dog got a chicken hanging around its neck?" Michael explained the dog had killed the chicken earlier that day hence he was trying to teach it a lesson. Albert retorted "I am sure it wasn't the dogs fault therefore take it off immediately" or words to that effect!

There was many a chuckle because that was how Albert saw it. No wonder he always said dogs make much better friends and are far more reliable than humans.

I gave the eulogy entitled 'Albert Spring - No Ordinary Man.' The audience liked it so now you can see where I got the title from. I hope you like it!

It was a tremendously proud moment. I had been determined we were going to give father the best send-off possible. There would be no regrets, as this was our last chance!

We like to think we gave him the send-off he richly deserved. We certainly were pleased with it all.

THE AFTERMATH

It took quite a while to go through all his papers, to write to all his contacts, sort out his various accounts which took time because we did not have the benefit of electronic systems such as email and the like.

Dan and I were executors to his will, which as is normal in such families had its moments, but we got there in the end.

Albert definitely had a sense of humour which showed itself through his will. In the period after Albert's death Mike Alderman asked me wistfully how it was going. After I explained to him we were dealing with the issues, he said Albert had told him "just watch the fun start when I have gone!" His mischievous sense of humour shone through beyond his days and to his grave.

His wish was for his ashes to be spread up Hamerton Grove in the company of his dear friends. Arthur, our brother and fellow Gamekeeper, duly discharged Albert's wishes with some of his closest friends. He is at peace there where he can keep an eye on his domain!

PERSONAL REFLECTIONS

It is strange to think how a short visit to those people in the Netherlands back in 1991 could have such an impact upon me.

Up to that point Albert was my dad. As I have alluded to he was, I suspect, a lot like many other fathers, doing their very best to look after their families.

There was not much love shown because that wasn't how it was in those days of austerity after the war. We were not treated badly, there simply wasn't a great deal of open affection. We had to earn whatever it was we wanted.

For whatever reason there wasn't a great deal of brotherly love between us four siblings. Being the youngest didn't make it any easier and as I now understand that is how it is with the four brothers in the one family.

But what I do know is that both our parents did their very best to look after us. As the youngest, I feel I received more support from them than perhaps my three brothers did.

In hindsight, it is that old cliche of I wish I knew then what I know now!

Upon reflection, father must have suffered the after effects of what he had been through in those relatively short but ever so long and enduring six years or so of the war and the fighting he was involved in.

On a brighter note, Albert did have a liking for wrestling on the telly. Some of you will remember the wrestling programme on a Saturday afternoon led by Kent Walton. Albert enjoyed watching his favourites such as Big Daddy, Billy Two Rivers and Giant Haystacks. Every year he would vote for Mick McManus as the Sports Personality of the Year!

For those of you who remember those days that demonstrates his sense of humour!

After seeing my Dad in a new light as a hero, certainly to others I had total respect for not only what he had done but how he had responded to it. It takes a special type of person to stand up to all that and come out the other end apparently unscathed or unaffected.

I always saw our family as very ordinary struggling to make ends meet in a small insular village environment, just like many others. There, apparently, was nothing special about that.

With the passage and benefit of time, to reflect and absorb in more detail what both my dad and mum did for us in very challenging times, I realise they did a really good job whilst also coping with their own challenges.

No life time is perfect, hence, with the challenges they faced and how they dealt with them were normal if you can consider the post war years to be normal! In summary, they did their very best for us and that is all that matters.

As the saying goes, 'everybody is ordinary until you get to know them.' When you get to know them and their lives they become remarkable people.

Now I have had this chance to find out about them in more detail, both parents, Albert and Olive, were remarkable for entirely different reasons.

Albert is the obvious hero because of his war time exploits which this book focuses on.

Olive's story is a little different because whilst she wasn't out there fighting the obvious enemy, she was at home, holding the family together with the constant fear of receiving the news her husband was lost at any time.

Therefore, I am rightly proud of both of them for the different reasons. As I am very proud of my Granny Farrer and indeed Granny & Grampy Taylor, who equally, must have endured very tough times without any obvious complaining or moaning; they were all a breed apart.

I am so pleased I gave him the ultimatum, or should I say the opportunity of returning to Holland in 1991. It was a leap in the dark for me too and I am so pleased we took the initiative and we did it.

I have learnt so much, met so many remarkable people, enjoyed special occasions and formed so many special friendships and, as a result, has opened up a whole new world for me.

Taking that step has resulted in this book which would not have happened if father and I had not taken that ferry in May 1991.

For that I shall be eternally grateful.

Writing this book has also been a cathartic exercise, inasmuch we spend so much time living our lives, that we become so wrapped up in our own little worlds. This endeavour has made me take time to reflect on what a good job my parents did in shaping my life and giving me the essential values to get this far in this changing world and effectively being a better person.

Taking a more holistic viewpoint of the people mentioned in this book and involved with Albert during the war years, they became my heroes, because they were prepared to make that ultimate sacrifice so that we could be free. Therefore, I am eternally grateful for what they did for us.

It is so important we remember them all including Grandad Spring who we never got the chance to know.

That is why I always wear a poppy to remember these people especially my grandad and what they gave for us.

Strangely, as time goes by, bearing in mind it is eighty four years since Albert was conscripted and nearly eighty years since Arnhem, the stronger the bond becomes. I cannot explain it!

ALBERT'S QUALITIES

He was a man of his word. He didn't need it in writing. His word was his bond.

He gave much more than he ever took from life and he certainly didn't count the cost.

He was a man of action; he would rather be doing than talking about it endlessly. If he did talk about it there would be few words unless he was talking about his beloved countryside and all that enriched his life.

He was a modest man; as the Commando message said he must have been good because they didn't suffer fools gladly. Indeed, he did walk amongst giants, although he didn't realise he was actually one himself.

He was independent, he would not be beholden to anyone.

He was a disciplinarian, however, he treated everybody the same regardless.

He was very loyal to his friends; thoroughly enjoyed their company and did not take them for granted. He did not look for the rich trappings of life. He was a very humble man.

At the end of it all, despite his adventures, he was always that same country boy from the little village of Winwick where he lived his whole life except for those times away during the war.

The reference Albert received upon being demobbed in 1946 sums him up very well; it reads

"I have known Sergeant Spring for over two years. He is an intelligent, reliable and trustworthy NCO. His conduct is excellent, I would thoroughly recommend him for any type of civilian employment calling for trust, loyalty and resourcefulness. A first class man in every respect."

I like the reference to 'resourcefulness'. I wonder what that means!

OUR FAMILY

Our Mum Edith Olive Spring

Our mum, born on 19th April 1917, the eldest daughter of Chris and Emma Taylor, of Clopton, a village just over the Northamptonshire border. Her younger sister was Ivy.

She always preferred to be known as Olive as she was not keen on being called Edith!

Despite bearing four sons, she was a very hard working lady who worked on the land with the harvest, stooking the corn sheafs after the binder, hoeing the sugar beet and picking and riddling the potatoes. The farmers found her to be totally reliable and trustworthy, hence, called on her services regularly.

Olive was eight months pregnant with her second eldest when Albert was reported as Missing In Action at Arnhem in 1944.

Olive died on Sunday 17th September 1989, ironically the anniversary of the start of the Battle of Arnhem, some forty five years earlier.

Edward Spring (our Grandad Spring)

Edward was from Oundle and he married Edith Rose prior to going off to fight in World War I with the Northamptonshire Regiment.

He was killed in action on Tuesday 10th July 1917 and is buried at Spoilbank Cemetery just outside Ypres.

Dan and I were so proud to have taken part in the remembrance service at the Menin Gate to commemorate the one hundredth anniversary of his death.

Sorry there is no photo but we do not have one. He is the Grandad we never knew.

I sincerely hope you enjoyed Steven Headley's words following his excellent research earlier.

Granny Farrer

Granny Edith May Farrer was a humble lady who lost her husband Edward in 1917 and was left with three young children to bring up on her own.

Granny remarried to become Granny Farrer which we never thought any more of. She was our wonderful granny regardless.

She lived most of her life at Vine Cottage in Winwick without electricity, hot water or an inside toilet.

She never complained and it was always wonderful to share valuable time with her by the light of her fire of an evening.

The most wonderful cook who could conjure up something from nothing from her hearth with the cracked oven wall.

Granny Farrer was known as the blackberry queen who would be seen out picking them as they grew wild in the hedgerows before they were killed off with the dreaded pesticides.

Granny died on 28th July 1976 at the age of 81 and is buried in the church yard in Great Gidding where she lived with her son Vic after leaving Vine Cottage in Winwick. At least she enjoyed the joys of electricity, hot and cold water and a proper indoor toilet!

What a super humble lady who life did not treat kindly. A fine example to us all and always my super hero.

Granny & Grampy Taylor (Emma and Chris Taylor)

Our grandparents from our mum's side who lived in the main street in Clopton for most of the time as I can remember.

Again, they did not ask for much from this world and they served and worked hard for their village community. I can remember them being effectively the caretakers for the local school which was a good walk from their home.

Grampy loved his big garden and, like the people of his time, he fed his family from it. As they got older, I would cycle over the six miles or so of a Saturday morning, to cut their grass and do odd jobs for them. No money exchanged hands; my reward was a lunch of a lovely piping hot rhubarb crumble served with a tin of carnation milk. There was nothing finer.

Grampy was a quiet gentle man who had spent all this working life working with horses including travelling as afar as South America. It was so good to spend time with him.

On the other hand, Granny Taylor was razor sharp who never missed a trick. She knew what was going on before many others. The local Vicar had to be on his toes when visiting Granny.

Our daughter Emma is named after Granny Taylor, now you know where you get it from!

Granny, and Grampy, were big friends with Mr and Mrs Mitchell, the owners of Clopton Manor, and after Mr Mitchell died, it was a regular occurrence for Granny to be seen perched up alongside Mrs Mitchell and Alan, the Chauffeur come Butler on the way to Oundle or Thrapston!

If I remember correctly Grampy was 89 and Granny 91 when they passed. Their simple life did them no harm. What wonderful people who gave so much to this world. It is so good to write of and remember them.

Ivy & Ted Pullan (Aunty Ivy and Uncle Ted)

Sticking with my mum's side of the family, her younger sister was Ivy hence our Aunty Ivy who was married to Edward Pullan who we knew as Uncle Ted. They lived down in a small town by the name of Dursley in the heart of the Cotswolds in Gloucestershire.

They enjoyed their beautiful stone cottage there where we visited for our two week summer holiday accompanied by Granny and Grampy Taylor when we were younger. The town and the countryside were delightful for relaxing and taking lovely walks in to the hills. Uncle Ted always said they were proper hills compared to Winwick Hill!

With the exception of Arthur, us three other boys loved visiting, even when we were older, as Aunty Ivy spoilt us because they did not have any children of their own.

Vic Farrer (Uncle Vic)

Vic was the son of Granny and Ernest Farrer who never married.

He always looked after us boys and then our children from a young age. He would arrive at mum and dad's house always with bags of sweets as a treat.

As a young boy, I used to go with him to Huntingdon Races, because that meant he had to keep sober to look after me. Thinking on, I am not sure who was looking after who and it was long before I could spell the word chaperone!

He was very good at table skittles where he often won the prize of a pig at the local village summer garden fetes.

Us Spring boys learnt to drive with impromptu driving lessons with Vic out on the empty country roads around Winwick!

Vic died in February 1987 and is also buried in Great Gidding church yard.

John Spring

John was Albert's brother and there is always some debate as to who was the youngest.

John lived most of his life down in the West Country where he was an AA man of some repute. I call still see the photos of him in his uniform standing outside the AA sentry boxes.

During the war he served in the RAF hence he used to accompany Albert to a number of the re-unions. I understand the craic was good because of the relationship between the different Armed Services.

When John died I was honoured to speak at his funeral.

Grace Groom

Grace was the elder half-sister of Albert and John who married Teddy Groom and lived in Winwick opposite Vine Cottage and then nearby Thrapston.

Peter Charles Spring

Peter was born on 17th November 1939 and, as such, was the oldest of the Spring boys.

He like Albert, joined the Parachute Regiment (the 3rd Battalion) and served during the late 1950s and the 1960s seeing action in Aden. Dan mentioned he served with Mad Mike but I am not sure which one.

After he was demobbed, he worked in the brickyards in Peterborough before he married Sheila and moved to near Burton on Trent where they shared a daughter Melody who has kindly provided Peter's photo for this book. He worked in the breweries there for the rest of his working life before he retired.

Peter, sadly, died of prostate cancer on 30th November 2009 at the age of 70.

He enjoyed the nickname of Poggy affectionately known as Parachute Poggy from us when he was in the army.

Arthur Edward Spring

Arthur was born on 19th October 1944 almost a month to the day of Albert going to Arnhem.

He was the country boy, like Albert, and indeed undertook gamekeeping duties on an adjacent estate at Leighton Bromswold including Salome Wood. He was considered to be good at it, although in later life, he took up stone masonry for which he also enjoyed an excellent reputation.

In his time as a Gamekeeper he and Albert enjoyed an interesting rivalry given they were keen to protect their own on their adjacent estates in Hamerton and Leighton.

Arthur's nickname was Dingy. Do not ask me where that came from!

Arthur, sadly, died on Sunday 19th December 2010, at the age of 66, no age at all.

Daniel James Spring (Crow to his friends)

Dan was born on Friday 5th September 1947 and went to school at Winwick, Hamerton and then the secondary school at Sawtry where he left school at fifteen.

Dan spent most of his working life at the Listers grass drying plant and farm just up the Thurning Road in Winwick.

More latterly, he took up clock repairs and antiques. He is still working at the ripe old age of seventy six, with his own workshop, still creating all sorts of architectural metalwork. His work is first class.

Dan and I are still supporters of the Commando Association (previously known as the Commando Veterans Association) and its events at Fort William on Remembrance Day and at the National Arboretum in Staffordshire where, we are proud to say, there is a paver dedicated to Albert on the Commando Association's Memorial.

We also enjoy returning to Arnhem on a regular basis.

We are also members of the Friends of the Tenth, who do brilliant work in commemorating and remembering our heroes and family members from the 10th Battalion The Parachute Regiment from all those years ago.

Dan is married to Marie and they have two children, Lisa and Sarah, and one granddaughter Chloe who has also visited Arnhem with us.

Dan has lived in Winwick for most of his life after living in Hamerton for a while when he and Marie got married. Indeed, he and Marie live at 5 Thurning Road which is four doors up Thurning Road from the original family home on Thurning Road where their daughter Lisa and son in law Neil live.

His nick name was Jim Crow, given to him by our mum because his middle name is James. He takes great pride in still being known as Crow to this day. Indeed a local brewery has named a beer after him! Cheers Dan.

ALBERT'S FRIENDS & COMRADES

Jimmy Turner

Jimmy was a lifelong friend who lived in the next village of Great Gidding. They were schoolboy friends and remained so all their lives.

Dan tells me that Jimmy was in the Tank Regiment during the war for which father admired him so much because he said "a tank was a readymade coffin and you would not find me in one for love nor money."

They enjoyed each other's company with that special bond. Their favourite past time was a day's rabbiting bearing in mind this was how country boys supplemented their meagre income back in the day.

I don't think they were ever happier than when they were out around the fields together or regaling their tales over a glass or two of whisky in front of a warm fire!

A genuine friendship that lasted a life time.

Jim Edwards

Jim lived out towards Spaldwick and worked in the family transport business before setting up on his own.

Jim, like Jimmy, was never happier than when he was out on a shoot day with Albert. Normally, he would be using one of Albert's dogs for game retrieving duties, picking up as we know it.

Talking of those dogs, Albert would let Jim have one of his trained gun dogs on a shooting seasons loan, but somehow the dog remained with Jim for the rest of its life. It was a standing joke between them.

It was not always one way traffic though, because when Margaret Thatcher decided the common man like Albert could buy their council house, Jim helped him fund it, and, if you see the tarmac drive at 1 Thurning Road, then I can remember Jim turning up with some spare material from a local tarmacking job his company had been doing. To this day I can see Albert and Jim raking out and laying the hot tarmac together.

Jim and Albert loved their times away on the grouse moors where they enjoyed a few days beating or picking up with a glass or two of whisky of an evening.

Jim was always a favourite of mine because he was a big Peterborough United (The Posh) fan. Albert was not interested in football in the slightest because he could never understand how on earth anybody got paid for kicking a bag of wind about!

Therefore I would go and watch the FA Cup giant killing Posh through the 60s. He would treat me to away days at places such as Sunderland and Chelsea which I have never forgotten. Thank you Jim.

Jim was one of the kindest people on this earth and he and Albert were the best of pals. He was a real gentleman who is certainly not forgotten as I still have a photo of him with one of Albert's dogs in my house!

Jim Westbury

Jim was a real character who is detailed earlier in this book hence not too much here.

He was a Yorkshire man who served in the Kings Own Yorkshire Light Infantry (KOYLI) who after the war married a lady from Nottingham where he lived the rest of his life.

Jim worked in the Post Office where he was a union representative. Boy, Jim could talk, so I am sure the other side gave in on most negotiations.

Jim and Albert got along fine because Jim could fight therefore as you may recall he was the first person Albert looked for when the going got sticky.

Jim's rank was as a Private but he was father's right hand man.

Jim, and his daughter Rona, joined us on a number of occasions in Holland. Albert certainly enjoyed his company. Sadly we have lost Rona more recently.

Corporal Morton

A short but poignant piece about Corporal Morton. We were talking about the men who were part of his stick at Arnhem and when we got to Morton Albert said "a rather unique thing happened between him and I. I went to his wedding one Saturday and his funeral the next."

He was a very good shot so when the 10th was disbanded he was assigned as a sniper trainer and as Albert said he was observing snipers carrying out training and he put his head up out of the fox hole and, as I understand it, one of the snipers shot and killed him from eight hundred yards away.

How desperately sad is that? Clearly father had plenty of time for Morton. Again the absurdities of war!

Roy Duhamaeu

Roy was a Sheffield lad who was in the same company as Albert in 10 Para.

He was a character and was on the other aircraft as part of Bill Burgess's stick who did drop on the drop zone and got to fight in the outskirts of Arnhem.

Roy always used to rib Albert and Jim and whoever he could get his hands on, saying "we were bloody busy fighting the Germans while you were drinking tea with the Dutch." A bit of banter goes a long way in such troubled times.

I represented Albert at Roy's funeral where I was pleased to report he did have the mandatory Union Jack on his coffin along with his coveted red beret.

A tremendous character who, although partially blind, attended Albert's surprise eightieth birthday party.

Hans Vervoorn

What a special man, who I liked the very first time I met him in 1991. I have written about him plentifully earlier, hence, all I will say is, he was a top person and what a character. He knew what he wanted as the story about his preference for beer rather than whisky proves.

How many of us in our youth chose to go on the run rather than sign up for something we didn't like? Truly remarkable.

Please see my notes of my thoughts after attending his funeral.

I also need to speak of Hans' family. It would be remiss of me not to mention them because of the love and care they showed specifically to Albert and, indeed, all of us.

Wil Vervoorn

Wil is one of the kindest and most beautiful people I have ever met. The way she looked after us when we visited and the way she looked after Albert, in particular, was so special. Her kindness and warmth were truly remarkable.

Wil did not have an easy time during the war but she did not put herself first once.

We were shocked when Wil died unexpectedly and I can tell you this world is worse off without this remarkable lady.

Lieke Vervoorn

The eldest of their three children, Lieke is a really good friend who always makes it her business to meet up with us when we are over in the Netherlands.

We know her husband Rik and their son Wouter. They are also dear friends and it is always so good to share their company as we do.

Lieke is just like her mum and that cannot be a bad thing.

Majorke Vervoorn

Majorke is the one who took after Hans career wise, as she is highly qualified in the field of dentistry. I have a book that she wrote as part of her PhD from all those years ago with nice smiley teeth on the front.

We do not see as much of her now as she is a busy lady with her work and her family. However, I remember us putting the world to rights one evening. Again a huge character.

Tina Rodwell nee Alderman (Tilly to her friends)

You may remember Tina as the young girl from next door who would help Albert turn the honey extractor in his garage or simply go and spend time with him after our mum died.

If the truth be known, he will have told Tina more than he would ever tell us.

Young Tina, as I call her, loved those times. Her favourite person from Albert's tales is Joe Beet who, as we all know, finished up in the compost heap in Castellaneta in Italy!

Even to this day Tina refuses to call him Albert, it is always Mr Spring. That is how much respect she has for him.

To demonstrate her wicked sense of humour Tina, after one of our visits back to Arnhem, sent Dan, my son James and me a mug each with the message emblazoned on the side 'To my Three Wise Monkeys Love Tilly.' Sounds about right!

Tina has been with us to Arnhem on a number of occasions hence is very much part of our team. Also her beautiful daughter Ellarose also joined us. My greatest wish being that she could spend more time with us. That is how much we love and treasure her.

Thinking about it, maybe, Tina is the sister we never had!

Mike & Maureen Alderman

Mike and Maureen have been my mum and dad's neighbours for so many years I cannot remember. They have always been very kind to Albert and been on hand to keep an eye on him.

Tina (Tilly) is mentioned earlier. They also had two sons namely Jim and Martin who I must mention.

Jim was their eldest son who died far too early. When he was a young boy, maybe a baby, he called Olive "Ov" and it stuck. He would very often pop round or appear at the window for a chat and stay for an hour or two. Ov was his second mum. Rest in peace Jim you are certainly not forgotten.

The youngest is Martin, commonly known as Bruce. Again a larger than life character who was close to my mum and dad and is still in touch.

Oscar Jordan

Oscar was a long term friend of Albert's. If he ever had fox or badger issues then father was his man. They were great friends and were never happier than when they were out in the countryside.

Oscar and his family were from Little Staughton and were close friends.

Mervin & Tom Joyce

Father was a long term friend of the Joyce brothers. Tom lived in Sawtry and Merve in Hamerton where Albert was the Gamekeeper.

Tom was the part time keeper at Aversley and Archers Woods out Sawtry way and Albert, again, was his man when he had a wild life problem he could not solve or he simply needed some help or advice.

Merve was a right character; he would be out beating with us on shoot days which often meant being out early in the morning carrying out stopping duties which meant stopping the pheasants from running away as they weren't daft!

Merve would always play a prank on us but, rain or shine, he was a very reliable source of a sweet or two in our moment of need. Again, what a character.

Later on in life, as we got older, it would always be so good to catch up with Merve in the Fox and Hounds pub in Great Gidding of a Friday or Saturday evening.

Malcolm Houghton

Malcolm was a rarity because he was the local post man from Sawtry which meant because he was out and about in the countryside every day as part of his job. As such he was the one who kept an eye out for any suspicious activity such as possible poachers or illegal hare coursing.

He was also a damn good shot and loved nothing better than a day's shooting.

Irene Bruning van Zanten

Irene is the daughter of Johannes van Zanten who very much represents the van Zanten family. We have enjoyed her company since 1991. Indeed, we have enjoyed her company so many times because she genuinely cares about her family and the legacy of her father.

What strikes me most is her kindness towards my dad, especially on his last visit.

I am privileged to have visited her home in Tiel and very much look forward to the next time we meet with the welcome of that little hug and a kiss.

This lady carries the torch for the van Zanten family and she carries it extremely well.

Johannes van Zanten

Maybe I have said enough about Johannes in the general text however this man deserves another special mention.

He is the man who provided the leadership and direction under the most testing of circumstances. He must have been very special for Albert to have held him in the highest of regard after relatively brief times together.

He put his country before his family, however, he was doing it for the sake and future of his beloved family and his country.

Johannes made the ultimate sacrifice for the benefit of us all. That is why we always pay our very best respects to this great man.

OUR FRIENDS

Gerard Nieuwenhuis

Whilst not a veteran of our original return to Arnhem, Gerard is still instrumental in the organisation of the events to continue the all important remembrance of those involved with the local events in 1944 / 45 in the Neder Betuwe region of the Netherlands, focusing on Kesteren and Opheusden in particular.

Such events include the opening of the very special Remembrance park at Opheusden near to the crash site of chalk mark 697, the Burgemeester receptions, the remembrance events at the grave of Johannes van Zanten in the cemetery in Kesteren on the evening of 4th May followed by Dutch Liberation Day celebrations the next day, the 5th May, including the more recent reenactment of the River Waal crossing undertaken by Albert and his men.

A true gentleman along with his lovely wife Toos.

Bart Belonje

Bart is the man who wrote the book 'To Honour and Remember' for Andy and Kath Shurbourne who he met in Arnhem when they said they did not know the fully story of what had happened to Reg and his comrades on the 18th September 1944.

It is a really good book in both Dutch and English telling the story of aircraft chalk mark 697 and their subsequent escape in greater detail.

I am delighted to have helped Bart with further information after the publication of the first edition with the end destination in Boven-Leeuwen because there had been confusion during the preparation of his book. Perhaps this will be clarified in the second publication.

Bart is the man who designed the wonderful Remembrance Park in Opheusden. Thank you Bart for such a fitting tribute to everyone involved back then.

It is always good to catch up with Bart and his lovely wife Anna.

Conny van der Heyden

What a lady, who took on the ultimate challenge of writing a book about Johannes van Zanten entitled 'Ten Onrechte Beschildigd' which means Wrongly Accused in English.

Whilst it is in Dutch, I have had part of it translated into English, particularly a section where Albert got a mention.

Conny is also involved with a museum in the Neder Betuwe which we have visited where Dan donated some of Albert's maps from his time in the region all those years ago.

Liset Vos van der Ven

The lady I call our Angel of Arnhem. We first came across Liset and her son Jelle at the opening of the memorial to the men of the 10th Battalion at Burrow on the Hill near Somerby where they both were involved.

Similarly, when my partner Zoë and I visited Oosterbeek on a river cruise holiday in 2022, we were diverted but we were still keen to place flowers on Alfred Penwill's grave. Liset came to our rescue by sorting the best of flowers from Holland of course.

Thank you Liset you are a super caring person and a special thank you for keeping an eye on Alfred's grave. Albert would be impressed with your kind deeds.

Arjen de Jong

Arjen, the son of Fre de Jong, who I first met on our return to Arnhem in 1991. He is so supportive in remembering what happened all those years ago.

It is Arjen who dispelled my myth of his dad Fre being the quiet one. He told me the story of his dad riding his motor bike through the village standing on the seat!

It is always so good to see him and his family including his sisters who we have met.

Jan & Sophie van Velzen

What they did in maintaining the Hazenhof in keeping with how it was back in September 1944 is nothing short of a miracle even down to the names of the animals in the stalls within the keeping of their home. We are eternally grateful for the plaques adjacent to the front door and the entrance gate. What a special occasion it was when they were unveiled.

Jan and Sophie always made us feel so welcome.

Sadly we have lost Jan, he is certainly not forgotten, and it still so good to catch up with Sophie and their son Mike.

Thank you for the way you looked after Albert over the years as I am sure he saw the Hazenhof as like a second home.

Martien & Wijnie van Barneveld

Dan and I have known Martien and Wijnie through the Commando Association because of their attendance at the Commando Remembrance events at Spean Bridge near Fort William in Scotland.

Martien's father, also Martien, served at the battle of Arnhem. He was one of 12 Dutch members of No. 2 Dutch Troop, No 10 Inter Allied Commando who crossed the River Rhine many times. He trained in Wolverhampton England where I am sure Hans Vervoorn also trained.

We enjoy such good times with these two special people. I call Wijnie Her Majesty the Queen of the Netherlands!

Mike & Anne Hayes

Mike (Micheal to give him his Sunday best name) Hayes is the son of Arnold Hayes who was one of the Paras on chalk mark 697 way back then. Mike lives in Rochdale, not far from me. He called me a good few years back to introduce himself as he had been given my contact details by I think Hans Vervoorn when he was visiting Arnhem.

I was really pleased to confirm his father was indeed on the manifest that day.

Last but certainly not least, what can I say about Anne his beautiful wife. What a fabulous character, a typical northern lass who sadly we lost in early 2023.

Sleep well Anne you are certainly not forgotten.

Mike is a real character who loves his jazzy or, should I say, funky cars and his motor bike. Not sure what his mum would think!

Andy and Sandra Shurbourne

It is always good to see Andy and Sandra as part of the bond between us all. We met up with Andy when he was with his mum Kath in Kesteren to mark the special occasion of the publication of Bart's book especially for the Shurbourne family.

Hope to see you both in September 2024 for the eightieth anniversary of the battle of Arnhem. Andy has a passion for older vintage cars which he and his friend drive out at some of the commemorations local to Somerby. Hope I have spelt Shurbourne properly this time!

ALBERT GETS A MENTION

My greatest wish has always been to find my dad's name in a book about his involvement in the war. All I was looking for was some recognition for him. His name in one book was all I was after, so I could say yes he was there because it says so in this book.

I am delighted to report my expectations have been exceeded because he is featured in a number of books including

- **Desert Rise - Arnhem Desert The 10th Parachute Battalion in the Second World War** by Martin Peters and Niall Cherry with John Howes and Graham Francis.
- **Edward Simons Fulmer Knight in the Military Order of William** by Laurens van Aggelen. Laurens, I still treasure the copy you signed for me.
- **To Honour and Remember Reconstruction Crash Dakota 697 18 September 1944** by Bart Belonje.
- **Arnhem Umbrella Major Digby Tatham Warter DSO** by Neil Thornton where I get a thank you on behalf of Albert who said Tatham Warter did remember the names of his men.
- **Ten Onrechte Beschuldigd (Wrongly Accused)** by Conny van der Heyden-Versnel which tells the story of Johannes van Zanten.
- **Airborne Troop Carrier Three-One-Five Group** by William L. Brinson And The Voices Of The 315th Troop Carrier Group. Receiving a copy of this book is very much thanks to Laura Briggs from Sudbury, Massachusetts, USA who's grandad, as I mentioned before, was one of those extremely brave pilots from the 315 Troup Carrier Group. Albert even gets a mention in this book all the way from the USA!

- **Oundle's War by Michael Downes** detailing the small Northamptonshire towns contribution to the war effort ranging from the people from the renowned local private school there, as well as the likes of Albert, a relatively local man, for his contribution to the war effort. This book illustrates how many local people contributed in so many different ways.

Thank you, each and every one of you, for mentioning Albert. You cannot believe how good it feels to see his name and photos in print. I know he would not necessarily agree but he richly deserves his recognition and I cannot thank you enough for just that.

Mentioning photos, sorry there are very few photos of Albert in a red beret as a serving soldier. The only decent photo I have is of him on the front row when the 2nd Battalion The Parachute Regiment marched through London on 17th September 1945, the first anniversary of the Battle of Arnhem.

All the other photos are of father in his Commando days in various guises and in groups, particularly when he was in the Middle East and North Africa. I suspect he was rather camera shy!

When I look at those photos you can simply see the exuberance in his face. He was certainly up for the challenge.

It is fair to say Albert never did seek the limelight. Indeed he shunned it but I am so pleased he has received some. That is the least he deserves.

Olive, our mum in her later years

John Spring, Albert's brother,
Uncle John to us

Vic Farrer, he always brought
sweets as you can see here
with my daughter Emma

Peter, eldest son who was also a proud Para (3 Para) following in Albert's footsteps

Arthur, second eldest son born one month after Albert went to Arnhem. Also a Gamekeeper

Dan, third eldest on the right. Phil, left, the baby of the family, at Arnhem in 2023

Emma and James Arnhem 2019. My favourite photo of them

My grandchildren, right to left; Martha, Ruby, Juliette, Ethan, Logan & Sienna

Jimmy Turner, Albert's lifelong friend out beating on a typical shoot day.

They enjoyed their days rabbiting and telling many a tale over a whisky or two!

Jim Edwards with Flyblow one of the dogs Albert loaned him! He and Albert enjoyed many happy times in the shooting field and the grouse moors

Tina "Tilly" Rodwell (nee Alderman), an important member of our team who listened to Mr Spring's tales whilst extracting the honey all those years ago

Olive and Albert's 50th wedding anniversary on 17th April 1989

Albert Edward Spring: No Ordinary Man

1942   1945
X

In Remembrance and Celebration

of

ALBERT EDWARD SPRING

6th May 1916 to 26th April 2002

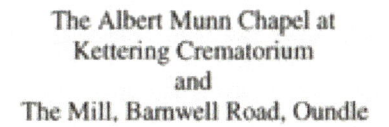

at

The Albert Munn Chapel at
Kettering Crematorium
and
The Mill, Barnwell Road, Oundle

on

Wednesday 8th May 2002

The day we said goodbye to Albert, certainly No Ordinary Man

Albert Edward Spring: No Ordinary Man

Albert, the country boy from Winwick,
as we will always remember him

ACKNOWLEDGEMENTS & BIG THANK YOUS

This book would not have been possible without the help and support of so many people, some knowingly, others unknowingly, over and above those I have mentioned already. I attempt to recognise those here. My humble apologies for any I have missed.

- The authors of the books noted earlier.

- Dan Spring, my only surviving brother, who has been an inspiration, think that is the right word, in terms of putting me right and coming up with gems of information that make this book worthwhile. He gave me honest and sincere praise for the first time during the course of this process. I have only waited seventy four years. Now that is some achievement and makes this book all the more worthwhile!

- The number of people who have said "you need to write these stories down" so many times including the last ones being Carey and Angela at Flora, our local garden centre, last summer, which triggered something in my head to go home and actually do something about it! Thank you Carey and Angela it was just the nudge I needed at the right time to get it done!

My proof readers namely

- Steven Headley, whose patience and research particularly on my Grandad Spring has been invaluable. He has a military background having served in the RAF as well as members of his family.

    Steve, I wish I had your patience and eagle eye for the detail. This very same man has also done valuable work on my family tree. Your encouragement and patience has been truly remarkable. Steve and his wife Helen, who I have known for forty years, are top people.

- Jeff Hewitt, who I came across through the Commando Association, is a retired Building Maintenance Manager for Thames Valley Police Force, who has co-authored two books, one being about his father who was a World War II Royal Marine Commando.

  Jeff has helped with the proof reading and presentation as well as providing much needed encouragement. Amongst his hobbies he lists enjoying a pint or two in his local and enjoys publishing awful jokes on his Facebook page! Thank you, Jeff and one day we will meet in person, maybe in your local, even if it is only to present you with your copy of this damn book!

- Elaine Jones, at our office, for her encouragement, help with the dreaded Microsoft Word and the reading of the draft. It was just what I needed. I hope we got the page numbering right between us.

- Liz Spring, for looking out all those old photographs and documents from Long Willows and taking Albert over to visit Ed and Lucille Fulmer in 1996.

- Zoe Kirk, my partner, for her proof reading and patience given my preoccupation with getting this book across the line!

Also thanks to

- Alan Orton and Phil Williams, who look after the Middle East Commando (MEC) Facebook page. The work these guys do is simply amazing. I could not believe finding random photos of Albert on their site over eighty years later. How did that happen?

- Jill and Mike Turner, for the chance to meet up again and provide the photo of Jill's dad Jimmy, Albert's lifelong pal. Thanks Jill and Mike, this book would not be complete without that photo and hopefully we can meet up again this summer. For the record, I have known Jill since I started work in 1967!

- To our friends from the Commando Association, (formerly the Commando Veterans Association) with whom we have enjoyed many occasions remembering our heroes at Fort William on Remembrance Day or at the National Memorial Arboretum at Alrewas. United We Conquer.

- To Alec Wilson, and his team at the Friends of the Tenth, who do such a great job of keeping the memories alive. I found reading Alec's book about his dad to be just what I needed when I was flagging. His dad was that man from the Pru!

- A special mention to my very talented 'Commando' sister Lorraine Smith. Thank you for listening and your advice and support. You are very special.

- To our dear friends of our own group relating to Chalk Mark 697 back in those few days in September 1944, who are mainly the children of our heroes from way back then. You know who you are and you are very special.

- To those children of the men involved who have been on this same journey namely Mike and Anne Hayes, Andy and Sandra Shurbourne and Rona Stevenson, Jim Westbury's daughter.

- Jan and Sophie van Velzen, who allowed us to share so many special memories at the Hazenhof, the 'home' of the Paras all those years ago. Your company and hospitality are second to none.

- Wil Vervoorn, who is such a hero of mine for how she looked after Albert with true love and care. What a special lady.

- Our Dutch friends whose acquaintance we have made and have become firm friends with such as Gerard Nieuwenhuis and his wife Toos, Bart Belonje and his wife Anna and Arjen de Jong. Also thank you to the leaders of the local communities in Kesteren and Opheusden who have made us all so welcome at those receptions over the years.

- We must not forget Nellie Silstra and the man with the jeep who presented Albert with the pieces of metal from aircraft chalk mark 697 all those years ago.

- To Laura Briggs, of the USAF 315th Troop Carrier Group, who is a fountain of knowledge about these very special band of brothers who gave so much.

  Laura is the granddaughter of Captain Paul Melucas, who was one of those remarkable pilots of the 315th TCG pilots, who actually took part in the delivery of the Paras of the 10th on the 18th September 1944. How special is that?

  Laura, thank you for the book where Albert gets a mention. Your energy and enthusiasm for this group is inspirational. And a big thank you to your grandad and his fellow airmen who we owe so much. I know they are your super heroes too.

- To our family members who have taken the trouble to join us on our visits back to Holland and with this book namely; Marie, Chloe, Emma, James & Olivia and Steven Ball, Sarah's boyfriend, and Melody, Peter's daughter. Thank you for your support and love. I sincerely hope you continue the special bond and remember and honour these very special people going forward.

And of course, our dad, Albert Spring.

Those men from September 1944, are our super heroes who will never be forgotten. Their bravery and courage at that time has allowed us to form a very special bond that gets stronger as the years roll by. Thank you for this special gift.

We cannot thank you all enough for all you have given to us and for adding to the heritage and quality of my life in particular.

INTERESTING MEMOIRS

This a collection of a few related memoirs you may find interesting relating to Albert's story. We start with;

Surrendering The Colours Of The 10th Battalion The Parachute Regiment by Phil Spring

In 1999 the 10th Battalion of the Parachute Regiment, then a Territorial Army Regiment, was disbanded and it was decided the colours would be presented to the Airborne Museum at the Hartenstein in Oosterbeek for posterity

When I got wind of this from somewhere I contacted the Regiment who kindly gave Albert and I invitations to the ceremony in Oosterbeek which included a blessing at the old church down by the River Rhine and then a formal ceremony at the Hartenstein presided over by General Sir Mike Jackson who was the Chief of Staff for the British Army. Mike is, of course, a well-known Para, who always wore his red beret and had seen some serious action particularly in North Ireland and as the leader of the Peace Keeping Force in Bosnia.

Cheekily, I asked for additional tickets for Hans and Wil Vervoorn and again they kindly obliged. I told you the Paras know how to look after their own!

It was a wonderful service at the beautiful old church, which is down the road from the museum going towards the river, where all the Paras gathered back in late September 1944 to make their escape across the river.

I was so pleased for father and Hans and Wil to be able to be there together. It was a proper military occasion that the British do the best. There was time for poignant photos of some of the original men of the 10th alongside the final current day members.

Then we sat and watched the final surrender of the colours in the grounds of the Hartenstein Airborne Museum to mark the formal end of the 10th but they will never be forgotten.

Our father Albert Spring was there at the beginning in Egypt and he was there at the end some fifty seven years later. How about that for devotion to duty.

It was very special.

I remember talking to the Officer at 10 Para, who organised the event, and I asked him what he was going to do next, to which he replied he was going off to undertake training for the SAS. That is what sets the men and, indeed the women these days, from the Parachute Regiment apart.

Phil Spring, feeling very proud.

Albert's Letter To Martin Peters Dated 12th July 1999

It is interesting to note Albert was 83 years of age then and not enjoying good health when he wrote this letter to Martin who was keen to understand about Albert's war time experiences. It was all written in his own handwriting, none of these computers in them days! I have transcribed it because you may not have understood it in parts. It goes like this.

Dear Martin

Thank you for your letter dated 23rd December 1998. I will give you the history of the original Tenth Parachute Battalion and how it came to be formed. There will be a lot of writing to complete it, but it will be done. One of my troubles is, when I have been writing for an hour or so, my hand gets cramp and so I just have to leave off; this, of course, is caused by 'old age'.

We will start on the 7th February 1940. On that day I travelled to Spring Hill Barracks, about a mile north of Lincoln City. This was the peace time base and training centre of the Lincolnshire Regiment and I was a conscript of what was known as 23 Group.

Right, I was in the army for the duration of the emergency, not at all unhappy about my situation. I was young, strong and very fit and I was a very good athlete and well able to look after myself in a fist fight, having spent a lot of hours sparring and such like in a gymnasium run by an ex-boxer named Jack Sharman, which was situated at Kettering some twenty one miles from my home. This was how it went; I would come home from work, have my tea, get on my bike and ride to Dalkeith Place that was the gymnasium, train hard for some two and half hours, including a road run and then bike home; I loved it. Twenty miles each way back to Spring Hill Barracks. Everything was fine, until suddenly the German Armed Forces woke up and it is all history now – Dunkirk came about and a tired exhausted B.F.F. was able to be brought back to this country, mainly through the gallant effort of our wonderful Navy and Airforce. Of course, Lincolnshire was now a frontline. Apart from Norfolk and Kent, it was closest to the enemy and enemy aircraft were part of the daily scene.

Almost overnight us trainees became trained soldiers, issued with live ammunition, trained to clean, prime and, eventually throw hand grenades, our favourite was the Mills 36. We were digging and constructing with sand bags all sorts of defensive positions ready for when the Germans attacked. We thought that they were sure to make the attempt, why they did not, we shall never know. We had been issued with Ross rifles; there were a good rifle of 300 calibre with aperture rear sight that was flipped up before sighting. These came back from Canada we were told.

One day in May, there was a notice on the daily order board, asking for volunteers for a specialist unit that was being formed. A number of us put our names down and then suddenly two hundred of us were told to pack our kit we were being posted to a Scottish unit as reinforcements. The unit turned out to be the Sixth Battalion Seaforth Highlanders – they had been very badly mauled at Dunkirk while serving in the 51st Highland Division.

Slowly by train we made our way to their Home Barracks at Fort George, then a couple of weeks later we were transported by train and lorries to Doune in Perthshire. This was a lovely place; it was a tented camp and, of course, we slept in bell tents, 22 men to a tent. Again, of course, we had dug in and sand bagged the floor of the tent in until we were two feet below ground level and when we laid down, the river flowed by only ten paces away; it was full of lovely fish.

This did not last very long; up on the board came a list of all the men who had volunteered for the Commandos. We packed our bags, were given ration cards, railway warrants for two weeks leave and ordered to report back to Netherdale Mill at Galashields in Peebles country, which eventually we did. There were 700 Officers and men mustered; we were examined, fed and issued with blankets etc.

I had a very good comrade who had volunteered with me at Lincoln T.T.C. – he was a native of Stamford and very hardy man, so, of course, we grabbed a double decker sleeping bunk and made ourselves at home. A couple of hours after we had arrived, our Commanding Officer who had marched with us, addressed us like this, his first word was "Gentlemen, you are all volunteers and, as such, you must be ready to fight against all tyrants and oppressors, so when we are welded into a well trained body of men, I hope it will be my privilege to lead you." His name was Lt.Col. R.N. Pedder who was from the Black Watch Regiment, who then told us that we were the Eleventh Scottish Commando.

The Commando was formed into 10 separate troops. Each troop was 52 Officers and men of the 52 in each troop. Once we were organised, there was a troop Captain a 2nd Sgt. in charge of each of two sections. The two sections were then organised into 2 sub sections, so the complete troop was a total of 4 sub sections, each sub section consisting of a Sgt, a Cpl, and two Lance Cpls. Each sub section was again split into three parts a Cpl in charge of the Bren gun team, a Cpl in charge of a rifle group, all qualified marksmen and the third group to act as reinforcements and carriers of spare ammunition etc., for the other two groups. They also carried a couple of grenade discharger cups; these cups were fitted onto the muzzle of a rifle which was loaded with a cartridge containing ballistic powder, which, when fired with the butt resting on the ground, would send the grenade a distance of up to one hundred yards; we made good use of these.

There were a total of 10 troops in the Commando – a specialist section of some 16 Officers and other ranks, who operated water cooled, belt fed, medium machine guns and a mortar section who operated the heaving mortars, consisting of four 4 inch mortars, capable of firing bombs a maximum of thirty eight hundred yards. These weapons were not very mobile; for instance, the barrel of a 4 inch mortar weighed 120lbs and the base plate 122lbs – but they were good weapons. Then there was the Battalion Head Quarters Ground who did all the administration and the total was 600 persons, or thereabouts, to complete a Commando.

So, we trained hard and well for almost a year, then we were put aboard three well equipped ships that we had been using in our training; these were the Glen Gyle, Glen Roy and Glen Hearn. All this was done at night in Lamlash Bay on the Isle of Arran. Each of these ships was equipped with A.L.C's (Assault Landing Craft).

We set sail. On board the Glen Roy was the 11th Scottish Commando, on the Glen Gyle was the 6th English Commando and on board the Glen Hearn the 8th English Commando – these had trained somewhere in England. The whole force was commanded by Lt.Col. Laycock and was code named 'Layforce'. The Glen boats were very fast, capable of 28 knots and we set out at night and by daybreak were out of sight of land and the sea was very rough; a great number of men were sea sick, but, sick or not it was training for us, weapon training, compass training, physical training, medical training, navigating by the stars, map reading, etc. We were also told that our destination was Egypt, which was a neutral country. We docked at Cape Town to refuel; it was a lovely looking place and would have loved to have seen more of it.

We arrived in Egypt and went to a fairly comfortable camp, built of mainly concrete slabs, but it was well equipped – a well furnished lounge and bar, even a library. Of course, it was a peacetime barracks for our forces when we were in command in Palestine and part of the treaty zone that covered a five mile strip each side of the Suez Canal. Our base was Kabrit; this was the place where the First Special Air Service was formed. The now famous S.A.S. Lt.Col. David "Jock" Stirling was the Officer in charge.

This was January 1941 and we were put into intensive training and our commanding Officer Lt.Col. R.N. Pedder was destined to lead us. The S.A.S., at that time, had a Special Boat Squadron; this usually operated from a submarine. They had a mobile Long Range Desert Squadron which operated at that time from Bedford short wheel base trucks and the vehicles were very carefully prepared for extremely rough travelling, equipped with four wheel drive and specially reinforced suspension. All glass and anything that reflected light was carefully camouflaged. We carried very large camouflage nets for camouflaging our vehicles whenever we hid up during the hours of daylight. Our armaments consisted of two Vickers K303 calibre machine guns; these were mounted on the metal upright on the passenger side of the vehicle. In the back was a browning .05 calibre which is half inch which was on a mounting that gave it a 360 degree area of fire; also it could be used against aircraft.

I was fortunate enough to be on a couple of the four week patrols; I loved it. There was a wonderful variety of wild life in the western desert. There were sand plover and wild turkey, a lot of gazelle, these usually weighed about 30lbs and, of course, snakes and lizards, also foxes.

So the month of May came and the Germans Airborne Forces attacked and captured the island of Crete. Unfortunately, the two English Commandos had been put on the island to help defend it. The Eleventh Scottish also set sail from Alexandria to be landed on the island, but unfortunately we were recalled while we were still aboard ship. We were aboard Lord Louis Mountbatten's destroyer, The Kelly. We were under air attack from the German Airforce at all times. I think we were very fortunate to survive. We then made full speed for Alexandria and were out ashore. The Kelly was refuelled, re-armed and returned to Crete to see if they could evacuate any troops but, by that time, the island was lost to the Germans and the Kelly was sunk by their Stuka dive bombers.

We are slowly getting to how the 10th Para was formed. Several days later our Commando was put on board a Glen boat and under escort we were landed on the island of Cyprus. At this time, the island was a British Mandate; our orders were to construct defensive positions and train the Cypriots to form Units similar to our Home Guard; this was very successful. The reason that we were put on Cyprus was our Higher Command thought that the Germans would try to take Cyprus and then Syria and the Lebanon – these two countries were already under the control of the Vichy French. Crete had fallen in the first two weeks of May and our High Command thought that the Germans would attempt to capture Cyprus and then join up with the Vichy French Forces already holding all of the Northern end of the Mediterranean Sea but the Germans had lost a lot of their finest Officers and men in the battle for Crete. Also, through the generosity of the United States our forces were building up their fighting strength. The United States, through a plan called

Lease Lend, sent us tanks, aircraft, lorries and even beer; I can remember it now, pint bottles of Dow and Black Label; it was very strong stuff and it was a present from the people in America who worked in the factories that built the lorries.

In May of 1941, the 6th Australian Division had arrived in Palestine. The object was to advance along the coast road and to drive the Vichy French out of the Lebanon and Syria; this was not going to be easy. It was very good terrain for defensive fighting, being very rocky; some of the boulders were large enough to hide a jeep. Everything was very quiet, the Australians advanced from Haifa, then they came up against the first natural defensive position which was the Litani river. The iron bridge was still intact, but the Vichy troops had cut out positions to cover the road where the Australian forces were jammed on the one vehicle width of track. The Vichy troops must have had thirty French 75's concentrated on that bridge and road. The banks of the Litani are some two hundred feet above the bed of the river, so of course, it was stalemate and it was like that for several days. Then it was decided to attack from the sea and capture the bridge from the West side. This attack was to be carried out by the 11th Scottish Commando, so we were briefed and we landed at 0900 hrs on that rocky shoreline; it was 7th June. This was the first and only time Lt.Col. R.N. Pedder was to lead his Commando into action. He was killed in the first ten minutes of the battle. The casualties were very high; I believe the total killed was 176 and another 200 wounded, a number of whom died later. I was wounded in the left thigh, with a piece of shrapnel; one of my men put a dressing on it and I just carried on as best I could; there was nowhere to run to. In 1943 I was fortunate enough to pass that way again and a comrade, Q.M.Sgt. Knobby Clarke took a few photographs of the graves.

Right, shortly after this, we had again been established in the training Headquarters at Kabrit. We were still Commandos wearing Battle Dress and Tam o' Shanter headgear, complete with bobble and Seaforth cap badge. We were comfortably housed in our same quarters at Geniefa, but now we were feeling rather dispirited because we had lost so many good comrades in the Litani river incident. The only consolation was that it was a success, but the battle was still in progress; it was to take the Australian Division three months to take the whole of that Syrian coast road.

Our barracks at Geniefa were no more than a stone's throw from Kabrit.

Then a rumour started, that our High Command intended to form an independent Parachute Brigade, its Headquarters at Kabrit. This rumour became fact and the forming began in the third week of November 1942. It was to consist of three Parachute Battalions and Brigade Headquarters;

It would be known as the 4th Parachute Brigade. The Battalion would consist of 10th, 11th and 156 Battalions; the 156 Battalion was already formed and would join us in due course which it did; it had been formed in India.

Right, the 10th Para was formed. Before I go any further I would like to tell you a couple of incidents. While we were still in the Commando a raid was carried out off the coast of Bardia, enemy occupied territory. Twenty two Officers and men were involved. We landed from a submarine, taking a lot of explosive etc., with us. Everything was ok no sign of Italian or German forces, so we marched quietly along the coast road towards Bardia; then we heard engine noise; it was a motor cyclist coming from the direction of Bardia. We went to ground on each side of the track. We had plenty of cord with us; this should have been out across the track to pull the rider off but it was not done. Somebody threw a grenade but the motor cyclist was twenty yards down the road when it exploded; he just kept going. We were a mile from Bardia; it took the rider a couple of minutes to get there and raise the alarm. In the meantime, we left the explosive and scrambled into our folboats and paddled as quickly as we could for the submarine. The enemy were driving up and down the track; fortunately their headlights were partly blocked out and we reached the submarine and made good our escape.

The second incident was the Rommel Raid. The objective was to capture or kill him,

The Intelligence Officers of the Eighth Army stated that General Rommel's Headquarters were in a villa on the outskirts of Bengahgafi. This was 200 plus miles behind the German front line position but it was decided to make an attempt to capture or kill him. Understand that General Rommel's brilliant and courageous way of leading his highly mobile Africa Corp had allowed the Eighth Army to regard him as invincible, which meant that the morale or the whole of that force were very disheartened.

In the early stages of the war in the desert, our forces had advanced right up to Bengahgafi and captured half a million Italian troops with hardly a casualty whilst so doing, but it was a different story when the Africa Corp arrived with their ME 109 fighter aircraft and their ME 110 fighter bomber. This gave them absolute air superiority, both in speed and fire power. Every day they would come, often 100 planes in line ahead. Mainly their objective was to bomb vehicles like lorries, Bren gun carriers and any of our tanks. The troops were used to their tactics and often dug trenches in advance, which at least kept them fairly safe. At that time we did not have many effective anti-aircraft guns; that kind of weapon was still needed in London and the large Cities and all along the Channel coast but our time was to come and then it would be our turn.

And so, our time did come. The Eighth Army, always led by the 7th Armoured Division, were advancing, only to be counter attacked by the then General Rommel's Africa Corp. The Africa Corp was highly mobile, with an abundance of tanks and self-propelled artillery pieces; their deadliest weapon at the time was the 88 millimetre gun. This weapon was highly mobile and fired a very high velocity shell; we soon got so that we recognised the sharp sound of an 88 when it was fired and, of course, they had absolute air superiority with their Stuka dive bomber, but we in the Eighth Army were learning more about how the Germans operated. We were becoming very experienced soldiers and all the time the Eighth Army was getting a slow but sure build up of tanks, mainly Crusaders. These were a very good medium tank and when they came equipped with a 17 pounder gun, then they were a match for any of the enemy's tanks: also for a start, we were getting a very useful fighter aircraft, the Kittyhawk. This aircraft, I believe, came on lease from America. Anyhow, the scene and pattern of the desert war was changing. Hundreds of Kittyhawk aircraft, 6 pounder anti-tank guns, 17 pounder anti-tank guns and the most important thing was the experts who came with them and very quickly trained us to use them: our morale was getting better and better. We had been through a terrible time in the Western Desert, with our backs to the wall when the Africa Corp had driven us completely out of Libya and we had dug in to make a last stand in Egypt, a neutral country, but we knew that our turn was to come. Then, of course, General Montgomery came and took command and he straightaway told us 'from this day on, the only movement will be forward' and, of course he was right.

What the then General Bernard Montgomery had told us, that the only direction that we would be going was forward, was absolutely correct, for the simple reason that he would not make a determined attack until he had an overwhelming force of aircraft, tanks and artillery under his command and, in due course, this came to pass.

In the waiting time, we carried out a lot of patrols, mainly to try to obtain as much knowledge as we possibly could of the Africa Corp's numbers and their armament. During the break up of the Commandos, we had been made members of the First S.A.S commanded by Lt.Col Jock Stirling. We did a Parachute Qualifying Course with the S.A.S at Kabrit and gained our wings. Then in November of 1942, the Tenth Parachute Battalion was born. We were given the opportunity to join it; this we did and so The Tenth Battalion was born.

We were soon in action. Firstly it was a few coastal raids, usually from a submarine; again to gain information of the enemy's strength and armaments, then in 1943 we were put on board the Battle Cruiser The Penelope at Berta In North Africa and crossed the Mediterranean sea to Taranto. This was on the evening of September 8th. The Italian Government had capitulated at midnight and so we sailed right up to the quayside and we were ashore, led by our Platoon Officer, 2nd Lt. W. Burgess and not a shot was fired. We went at the double and took up positions covering all roads and buildings that might be occupied by the Germans but the Germans had abandoned the Port completely. There were groups of Italian Servicemen about; they still had their weapons but they made no threatening moves towards us, so we walked straight up to them and saluted them. They seemed surprised but they returned the salute and we shook hands all round and the tension was gone. They were quick to inform us that they were now our allies; they also informed us that all the Germans had gone and there were not any booby traps or mines in the area. This information was very useful to us; we found out that it was correct. They also informed us that the last Germans had left during the night and had gone on the road that led to the Port of Bari, so we had to cross right across the heel of Italy and the German troops were the Hermann Goering Parachute Regiment, so we knew that their armament would be very similar to ours.

Now this German Para Unit was just fighting a delaying action, to allow the German infantry and Light armoured units to evacuate their vehicles and armour at the deep water Port of Bari and they made a fairly successful operation of it.

Now we were at Taranto and there was no opposition, so we force marched to the nearest village, some nineteen kilometres *on the road to Bari. We got into the village Massafra without firing a weapon. The Italians informed us that all the Germans had left in a great hurry and they had not observed them laying mines or booby traps. We found out that they had told us the truth, so we put out our listening posts with their short range transmitting wireless sets and rested for the night. The next village was Piagliano; this was some seventeen kilometres from Massafra. As soon as it was light and we had some food and washed, shaved and seen that our weapons were in good order, we prepared to advance. We were in very low ground; it was a good defensive position but we had to attack uphill all the way and the moment we prepared to advance, we came under persistent heavy mortar fire and machine gun fire. It was here that our General, General Hopkinson was killed. He had joined us to observe how the battle was going and he had walked up the road with an American Liaison Officer, a Col. Grant Taylor and he had been hit by two machine gun bullets, one in the chest and one just under his right eye. I know, because the two medics who carried him back into a sheltered position, put him down close to us while our medical Officer, Capt. Drayson, examined him. Capt. Drayson was a very good medical Officer and he was, I am sorry to say, killed at Arnhem in September 1944 – I have a photograph of his grave.*

Now the next objective was Castellaneta; we could see it in the distance. It was at least 1000 yards higher than we were and although we were unaware of it at that time, it was the battle to take this place on which the whole of the offensive depended. We came under very heavy mortar and machine gun fire but we were getting a lot of support from our own mortars and heavy machine guns. Sgt. Bently was our Sgt., organising our mortars and he was very efficient at all times. His mortars were capable of a range up to just under 400 yards; of course, an Officer was in overall control of Sgt. Bently's team.

In the advance, a number of men were wounded by shrapnel but none of them really seriously and so we got into the town and we had no opposition; in fact the Italians rather hindered us by coming out and offering us food and flowers; the food was always boiled macaroni with tomatoes in it; it was alright but we were too busy to enjoy it.

So we got into the town; it was a natural defensive place. We had got into the south end and we prepared to advance north. On the right were houses, on the left a stone wall – no grass verges, just had road, well maintained. The height of the wall above the road level was some 4ft but on the other side it was a sheer drop, varying from twenty to thirty feet. All was still at this time, so we advanced section by section. We reached the stone water trough and several small trees; there was a road that went off to the right and at that point a machine gun opened up from our immediate front and another from the side street. We did not have any real cover and two of my men were hit, one of them a young soldier, his surname was Martin; he always looked so boyish and young, that we always called him young Martin; he died during the night. The other wounded man eventually made a good recovery and came back to the unit after we returned to England – that is war and that is how it goes. When we were ambushed, the first man to get his machine gun into action was Jim Westbury. This was to be the last really serious fighting.

Our next objective was Goirya, a small town, we attacked it and were driven back by a quick counter attack but we went in again and captured the place, and a fair amount of rations and ammunition that was loaded on an Italian Flat lorry that had broken down. Some of our mechanical minded men got it going again, so we took it with us; it came in very useful. We pressed on to Bari to be met by the Italian civilians, including the Lord Mayor who gave us a great welcome. The Germans had evacuated the city and declared it an open town, so at last we could wash our clothes and check all our weapons, have a bath with hot water and plenty of soap; it was surprising how much better we felt.

We stayed in Bari in luxury and comfort. Of course, we were actually briefed for a seaborne attack on the shore of Foggia but our heavier units advance more easily and quickly than they expected; we thanked them in our minds and toasted them in wine, which was cheap enough. It was possible to buy a hogs head of rose and red wine, the barrel contained 72 gallons for just 3 pounds sterling; I know, because the Comfort Funds Officer used to buy one for the whole unit.

After a month, it was back to Taranto and home to England, landing at Liverpool on the 19th December 1943. Little did we think of the carnage that we were to be sent into in the following September in Arnhem. That was the end of the Tenth Paras campaign in Italy.

You know all about the Arnhem Battle, so now you know it all.

You have my permission to use all or part of what I have written but do not change the actual facts.

Signed

ALBERT SPRING

Hans Vervoorn's Funeral My Thoughts

These are my recollections of the occasion of the funeral of Hans Vervoorn on 5th October 2012. It is important to remember I made these notes as I travelled back from the Netherlands to Ireland to visit my son James. Hope they make sense.

I arrived at Han's apartment in Voorburg, where it was good to be greeted by Lieke & Marjoke. Lieke asked if I would like to see Hans, he looked so peaceful.

Wouter and I went to the flower shop & bought a nice bouquet on behalf of Mike & Anne Hayes and my family.

It was great to see Hans junior as it has been a long time. This must be a very difficult time for him. It is gratifying to learn he has been visiting his father on a regular basis.

Met Marjoke's girls, Maud and Anna Mieke plus their pals on the way.

The undertakers were at the house when we got back. They brought Hans out of the bedroom, as is the Dutch way, and then with the help of the family put him in the coffin, along with a flower from each member of the family. I helped screw down the lid.

We then chatted for a while before travelling to the crematorium in convoy following the hearse.

Travelling with Rik and Deidrick is always good because we indulge in catching up on the latest art deals, and the state of the Dutch economy and politics. It is important to remember that it was Deidrick behind the reunion of 1991 after all.

There we, socialised and I met Hans's brother Dick, and his wife. Hans half-brother was also there. I had not realised his mum had died when he was 14. The grandchildren were there and there was lots of kissing, remember they kiss on the cheek three times not two!

We were then invited to go through into the main auditorium where Hans's coffin was resplendent draped with the Dutch flag. Father would have been happy about that! There was also a picture of Hans out front and plenty of flowers.

There was a simple funeral service card for everyone.

The auditorium was full of the family & friends in the front row, where I was privileged to be sat.

Lieke commenced the proceedings with an emotional address the bulk of which was in Dutch. I could follow the gist but not all.

A gentleman with more medals than you could shake a stick at spoke of Hans's war record and whilst in Dutch he spoke of Hans being awarded the Bronze Lion for his efforts at the time of Operation Market Garden. He stood to attention as he faced the coffin. Clearly a mark of respect for a remarkable veteran.

Then it was my turn, starting with reading Mike Hayes's letter addressed to Marjoke, Lieke and me. In talking to people afterwards they recognised that tears were not the sign of weakness but perhaps a strength after all.

My speech was easier because it was from the heart and with true feeling. In talking to people afterwards the coming together in 1991 was clearly cathartic for both Hans and Albert because it gave them new purpose in their more senior years.

After speaking at my Dad's funeral ten years prior this was just as gratifying and you know when you have done a good job when people tell you how much they enjoyed it.

I felt I had done justice to Mike & Anne Hayes, Hans, Wil, Albert, Lieke, Marjoke, Hans junior, their families and the great Dutch people.

Followed by Vera Lynn singing "Land of Hope & Glory" - very touching

The grand children were magnificent; the bond between each of them and their grandad was clear to see. Tears flowed but what do you expect as this was their final farewell and Hans would understand anyway.

Marjoke read out an address from the hospital in Uganda which Hans & Wil sponsored. Indeed a Mass was held for him the previous evening. Their respect and appreciation for what he has done for them is clearly greatly appreciated.

Vera Lynn then sang "We will meet again"

There was also a recording by a Soweto choir

At the close everyone filed past the coffin and photograph to say their last farewell to a truly great man.

Irene, the daughter of Johannes van Zanten, was there and it was wonderful to shake her hand and give her a kiss. A wonderful lady from a great family who gave so much to the cause of freedom.

We enjoyed a light reception at the crematorium where I talked to a man called Paul and his wife who's name I cannot remember but was a Doctor. They met Hans in Indonesia and recalled their time with him and Wil. Paul was in the diplomatic corps and said Hans was a clever man who knew how to find a way round the vagaries of diplomatic and political life.

They told me Hans left Indonesia in 1974 to go to Africa.

I regaled them with the stories of Hans & father's time together which Paul said I should write down otherwise they will be lost forever.

We then travelled back to Hans & Wil's apartment in Voorburg for a final gathering over a drink and nibbles.

Lieke said a few words of appreciation and how much her father would appreciate everybody being there. Clearly it was an emotional time for Lieke but she coped extremely well and Marjoke has provided brilliant support.

I must say that Marjoke showed a wonderful way with the children at the crematorium when it was emotional for them. Marjoke has a similar style to that of Hans & Wil. Could it be the medical training in her?

The closeness of the Vervoorn family throughout has been striking.

When I last spoke to Hans on 18th September 2012, he remarked how well the girls and their families had looked after him.

Lieke spoke of her time sitting with her father at home and talking through all those issues from times gone by. I think that has proved good for her.

Clearly not having Hans there will leave a big void in their lives but they can be very proud of their superb efforts.

As one of the speakers said most people are granted 70 years life (three score years and ten) and given that Hans was granted 89 years shows of his contribution to mankind. A great man.

It was a privilege to have a chat with Dick, Hans's brother and to ask him what sort of brother was he. Dick said Hans would advise him on his girlfriends and would always recommend those girls with double barrelled names.

I spoke to a lovely lady who is a teacher who was keen to know about my dad and his time with Hans.

Similarly, there was the son of Hans's sister who had recently revived the family get togethers that Hans had organised many years ago.

Indeed, he told me the last such event had been held two weeks ago and Hans was talking of how to celebrate his 90th birthday. Life can be cruel sometimes!

This particular gentleman is keen to continue with the family gatherings.

He was also interested in the book Harry Tomeson had written about his time in the war. I told him that I had a manuscript in English which Hans had translated for my dad. I gave him my card so he can email me his contact details whereupon I can send him a copy.

I did say it is in Hans's best doctors writing so it may take some time!

A number of people asked why it took so long for my father to return to Holland after the war.

It is simple; the war leaves many scars and my father, like so many others, just wanted to return to a normal life. It is so important to realise war times are far from normal for fellow soldiers and their families.

Given that my father had been away fighting for five years whilst leaving a wife and two children at home he had realised that war was futile and for once Churchill was right it is better to "jaw jaw than war war". Father also realised the Germans were a worthy foe and it was difficult to see an end to this damn war.

When you analyse the facts of aeroplane 697, that fateful aircraft that crash landed in Kesteren, two American aircrew lost their lives and one Para was killed on the drop and ironically one other was killed on his way to hospital in Nijmegen. In total 4 people lost their lives out of a total of 20. That is 20% loss rate for what was a simple mission.

As I reminded myself and others at the funeral of the 580 men of the 10th Battalion of the Parachute Regiment who left England that day only 43 returned. The others being either killed, injured or taken prisoner.

We must never forget the sacrifice the Dutch Resistance made, and, of course, Johannes van Zanten's name comes to mind. A difficult situation for any father of 5 to make

If I understand the situation correctly, Hans was a student at the time of the German occupation and was asked to sign an allegiance to the Nazi cause. He refused to do so, hence his underground days were born. How big and difficult decision is that?

I cannot help but remember that this war cost Britain two million lives in the name of freedom. We do not realise how lucky we are not to face such ultimatums in our life time.

It was then time to say farewell.

The grandchildren, of course, were in the kitchen area. They are good people and have so much adventure before them and I am sure they will do well.

I shook Hans junior's hand and it was truly good to see him again. May life be kind to him.

I kissed Marjoke and wished her well. This lady is very much at ease with herself and reminds me of both Hans and Wil.

Lieke is a really focused lady, who carries the burden of being the eldest sibling with a determination to do the right thing. Lieke, with Marjoke, certainly has done just that. Her father would have been so proud and wholeheartedly approving of the occasion and its organisation.

And finally a good shake of the hands of Rik and Deidrick, who feel like soul mates and it is always good to be with them.

Then I am on my way back to the airport for a flight to Ireland to join my son James and his family.

On reflection the thoughts that come to mind are;

 # Hans and Albert's friendship was born out of adversity and built on mutual respect.

 # Hans Vervoorn has been a beacon to me and is a perfect role model on how to live.

 # I would not have missed this occasion for the world.

 # Hans, Wil, Father and the other great American, British and Dutch people involved will not be forgotten.

 # The friendship of the various families will continue as a mark of respect for what their parents stood for in thought and deed

A Tilly Moment by Tina Rodwell (Nee Alderman) commenting on an early draft of this book

Having spoken of my dear friend Tina Rodwell and her many talents I have decided to add one of her many Tilly Moments. I hope you enjoy her beautiful words written after looking at an early draft of this book.

I hope I have done justice to Tina's excellent advice and suggestions.

Hi ya,

Well done on the next draft, will make time to read with my dogs and coffee. A very special time that you have given me, so thank you.

I'm dyslexic so am a slow reader and, rule of thumb, I always read 3 times. 1 reading always the slowest as I make notes. 2 is for do I agree with my notes lol 3rd is so I have the right notes and have I got the right idea. That's on my own writing and when I'm asked to read other people's work I hope that is ok?

I like to leave a gap between each read so that I know I'm reading it right, being dyslexic I think I'm reading it right but not always. I'm yet to do 3rd reading and was going to look up a few dates for you.

I think this telling of Mr Spring's life is very important I wanted to know about your journey from boy to man. I wanted to hear your voice less controlled and more personal. You have a good writing voice so use it.

Mr Spring enabled you to grow through his experience and the people you met through his adventures and what you have passed on to your family and friends. This I think is the story readers will want to hear and make Mr Spring come alive in their lives.

When did you learn about his hardships in boyhood, his writing or his telling or by someone who knew him back then and talked about it. Readers want to know how you found out and how it felt.

All the way through you give sound bites of a bigger more coloured story which in second draft you could work on. Writing I have to tell you is hard work with many drafts and edits.

Mr Spring knew Paddy. The chess game how was this told ?

Anyhow these are my first thoughts but need to read through to make sure I'm right. I hope you find the above thoughts helpful but let me know what you think.

I have a couple of heavy days with ME stuff, I give a speech tomorrow on the Disabled Charter and it appears the charity are determined to march to parliament again. Not sure how much difference it makes but you have to try. Mr Spring was right the people at the top are mostly fools that don't know the facts lack communication skills and just give out orders and when they are doing that I always see your dad's face winking at me knowing it will stir me into action.

Good Lord not sure I justify a mention xx

Tina xx

Milton Keynes UK
Ingram Content Group UK Ltd.
UKHW021139300924
448903UK00001B/9